# CHURCH LEADERS HANDBOOKS

# DIVORCE
## AND
# REMARRIAGE

## J. D. THOMAS

Published By
**BIBLICAL RESEARCH PRESS**
774 East North 15th Street
Abilene, Texas
79601

# DIVORCE AND REMARRIAGE

By J. D. Thomas

Copyright © 1977
Biblical Research Press

Library of Congress Catalog No. 77-91309
I. S. B. N.-0-89112-159-5

# PREFACE

The effort in this first volume published of a new *Church Leaders Handbooks* series is to furnish understandable and comprehensive aid to Church leaders who have to deal with problems of divorce and remarriage, and of course for those who may be involved in them.

To be sure the conventions of our society have become more liberal and open than at any time in the history of Christianity. The sexual revolution and the accepted mores concerning divorce and remarriage of our age are placing a tremendous pressure upon those who would please God in their lives. Those who do not know past history and are not careful Bible students become overwhelmed in a hurry as they face these problems. Some sin in ignorance and some perhaps willingly, but all sins need the cure of repentance and an application of the shed blood of Christ.

It is our hope and prayer that this study will be of help.

J. D. Thomas

# CONTENTS

# Chapter 1

## INTRODUCTION

There is no problem more serious today for church leaders and for those caught up in the problem, than that of Divorce and Remarriage. The problem, first of all, concerns the relation to God of those involved in it. This is the major concern of all, or should be. All want to go to heaven, but sometimes the sexual relationships of men and women bring dangers of not even being able to do that.

We plan to study in this book divorce and remarriage and what God does and does not approve, because "rightness" about the marital union itself should come before studying how best to make it ideal. There are numerous studies about marriage and how to make and keep it optimum, and these we recommend. But there are so many varied claims about what the scriptures do or do not teach about who is an eligible person to whom one can be married, that study in this area seems to be the first need.

Changes in the basic philosophy of our society, including that from a definite, positive, authoritative pattern of behavior for all humanity, to one of a completely subjective morality with each man serving as his own authority, have put tremendous pressures upon all marriages in western society, and Christian homes are not exempt. The sad thing is that God's word is not being taught or respected in America today to the degree it was in an earlier period, and many Christians are behaving like the rest of society. The temptation of sex is ever with us, and Satan is constantly alert to make the most of tempting us.

Divorce has risen so rapidly in recent years that now in some communities more divorces than marriages enter the public records in a given period. Only in those homes where the utmost respect for the Bible is held by both spouses does there seem to be a good chance of the marriage surviving. The will of God that there be "one man for one woman" does not seem to be understood in any significant way. Rather the social convention that divorce is easy and desirable if the marriage becomes a little unpleasant has come to be accepted. We might refer to the old illustration that if a man was marooned on an island with his wife, they would surely work out all problems. The availability of someone else is what makes most people not want to "work things out", and we follow the line of least resistance.

Admittedly the sex drive is one of the strongest, and without a very strong moral stamina it is easy for people to fall into the trap of sex-related sins. Love enters the picture also, since we find that in many of the adulterous unions with which we have to deal a tie of love has developed and it blinds those involved to reason and to a fair consideration of the will of God. When one is under a strong emotional influence, it becomes easy to rationalize. Self-justification seems to be about the easiest thing to do for most of us humans. The problem becomes further complicated if children are involved, and in so many cases it turns out that individuals are going to follow their own wishes regardless of truth or right in God's sight. Still further, there are preachers and other religious tutors who encourage people to sin and to do what they wish, arguing that the Bible doesn't really mean what it has been understood to mean. God's love and mercy are invoked, as covering sins even without repentance.

All this leaves elders and other church leaders in a difficult situation, for they are called upon to "watch for the souls" and to make decisions in such matters. These decisions are often weighty, since they do involve the application of the word of God to specific cases, affecting children as well as the involved adults, for all of their future lives. Responsibility for correct decisions bears down upon these leaders, and probably these are the most weighty problems that they have to deal with as church leaders. This calls for a thorough knowledge of God's word, and for experience and wise judgement in its application. Again, no two of these problems are exactly alike, and facts must be gathered to establish all the relevant factors in each case. It would take almost the

2

wisdom of a Solomon to solve some of these problems, and it is no wonder that the scriptures prescribe 'double honor" for those who carry responsibility for the souls of others in this way.

## Problem Areas

There are differing points of view about numerous questions for which we need to have a clear interpretation of the teachings of God's word. These varying understandings are often juxtaposed to bring unusual conclusions, and surely the method and often the motivation of most of them are wrong. They may be motivated by selfish considerations, albeit not recognized or admitted by the person holding the wrong conclusions. The present writer admits his own human limitations, and hopes that for any wrong views set forth here others will clarify and straighten out the teaching. Many of the arguments offered on these problems have to be clearly wrong, so we hope to bring truth to light on at least some of them. The problems include:

1. God's marriage law in each covenant, and how the covenants relate to each other.
2. How the teaching of Jesus relates to the teaching of Paul.
3. How human civil statutes relate to God's law.
4. The responsibility of today's alien sinner to God's marriage law.
5. The demands made by genuine repentance.
6. The effects of Christian baptism upon the alien adulterer.
7. The status of the guilty party in a "scriptural" divorce.
8. The obligation of the Christian if an unbelieving spouse "departs".
9. What elders should do as responsible overseers in such cases.

We trust the above problems and questions will be discussed with sufficient thoroughness to enable our readers to know what God expects of them.

## Definitions

A prime consideration of this study will be to decide what actually constitutes a marriage union in God's sight.

3

Human definitions do not matter, if they differ from what God considers marriage to be in actuality.

This writer has held that God counts a marriage to exist when an eligible man and woman "decide that they are married." This definition is flexible enough to not depend upon a human ceremony and thus includes "common law marriages." It also includes the union of Adam and Eve, for instance, or a present day union of an eligible, marooned couple on a desert island where there is no human law to apply, nor anyone to say a ceremony. In every case, of course, both parties would have to be eligible candidates for marriage in God's sight. This definition would not allow it to be a marriage if one of the parties were already married to some-one else in God's view, nor would it allow a homosexual union. It does, however, fit every "legal" marriage of what-ever society or culture one lives in.

Additional uses of the English word *marriage* in the New Testament with distinctive shades of meaning include: 1) A divinely approved marriage, where there is no question but that God sanctions the union (See I Corinthians 7:10; 39; I Timothy 5:14; and, 2) A marriage recognized and approved by man's law but disapproved by God and thus considered adultery by him (See Matthew 5:32; 19:9; Mark 6:17; Romans 7:3). Surprisingly enough the distinction between these two meanings is obvious on the face of it, but some writers on the divorce and remarriage problem apply the passages wrongly, thus claiming that God approved a certain relationship when in fact he counts it as adultery.[1]

Other key terms that demand definition and distinction in this study are "fornication" and "adultery."

## FORNICATION:

Webster's Seventh New Collegiate Dictionary:

for·ni·ca·tion \,fȯr-nə-'kā-shən\ *n* **1** : human sexual intercourse other than between a man and his wife : sexual intercourse between a spouse and an unmarried person : sexual intercourse between unmarried people — used in some translations (as AV, DV) of the Bible (as in Mt 5:32) for *unchastity* (as in RSV) or *immorality* (as in NCE) to cover all sexual intercourse except between husband and wife or concubine **2** : sexual intercourse on the part of an unmarried person accomplished with consent and not deemed adultery

4

New Interpreter's Dictionary of the Bible:

**FORNICATION** [םינונז, הנז; πορνεία; *etc.*]. The practice of sexual immorality and harlotry; hence a symbol for idolatry. In the OT it is equivalent to "playing the harlot" (Gen. 38:24; Deut. 22:21; etc.; *see* PROSTITUTION). In the NT the words for "fornication," "to practice fornication," etc., refer to every kind of sexual intercourse outside marriage.

Arndt and Gingrich—A Greek-English Lexicon of the New Testament:

πορνεία, ας, ἡ (Demosth.+; LXX, Philo, Test. 12 Patr.) *prostitution, unchastity, fornication,* of every kind of unlawful sexual intercourse.
1. lit. Ro 1: 29 t.r.; 1 Cor 5: 1a, b; 6: 13; Hm 4, 1, 1. W. ἀκαθαρσία 2 Cor 12: 21; Gal 5: 19; Eph 5: 3; Col 3: 5. Differentiated fr. μοιχεία (Philo, Mos. 1, 300) Mt 15: 19; Mk 7: 21 (WGabriel, Was ist 'porneia' im Sprachgebr. Jesu?: Ethik 7, '31, 106–9; 363–9); Hm 8: 3; D 5: 1 (the pl. denotes individual acts). On the other hand μοιχεία appears as πορνεία (cf. Sir 23: 23) Hm 4, 1, 5.

**ADULTERY:**

New Interpreter's Dictionary of the Bible:

adul·tery \ə-'dəl-t(ə-)rē\ *n* [ME, alter. of *avoutrie,* fr. MF, fr. L *adulterium,* fr. *adulter* adulterer, back-formation fr. *adulterare*] : voluntary sexual intercourse between a married man and someone other than his wife or between a married woman and someone other than her husband

From the above definitions we may say that *fornication* (the word in the "except" phrase of Matthew 19:9) means any and all kinds of illicit sexual intercourse or union (including homosexuality); while *adultery* simply means intercourse where one (or both) is married to someone else. Adultery is, therefore, one form of fornication, the latter being the generic term and adultery the specific. It is needful that these definitions be carefully kept in mind, because some strange meanings have been given to them apparently in the hope of justifying some unholy union.

Three observations should possibly be made just here:

1) It should be made clear that God holds that some women are "off limits" to some men. Deuteronomy 24:1-4 says that when certain conditions develop, a sexual union between the

5

wrong persons is an abomination to him. Christians should, therefore, be careful that they do not trifle with God's will, regardless of emotional ties that have been built up.

2) A Bible interpreter should recognize that he must not feel obligated to guarantee "a happy sex life henceforth" to everyone that asks his opinion about scripture. It may well-be that some people so conduct themselves that celibacy in the future is the only clear path open to them. Jesus indicated (Matthew 19:12) that some would do well to become "eunuchs" for spiritual ends.

3) The Bible only is our guide, and we must be willing to accept its authority above our own emotions and desires. Logic and the word of God must take precedence over emotion and even what might seem to be quite a satisfactory human relationship.

## STUDY QUESTIONS

### Chapter 1

1. Let the class comment on the present day plight of society with respect to sex and morals and the decline of respect for marriage.

2. Why should a study of God's teaching on marriage come before one on ways to improve marriage?

3. Describe the quandary of church leaders as they face the divorce and remarriage problem.

4. List problem areas to be covered in a study of this kind.

5. Define "marriage"; "fornication"; "adultery".

6. What is the danger of giving too much consideration to the appeal of the emotions?

# Chapter 2

# GOD'S MARRIAGE LAW NOW

In the beginning after God created Adam, he made Eve to be his helpmeet, and they clave together and became *one flesh* in a husband-wife relationship. Thenceforth marriage was the common practice, as the early chapters of Genesis indicate. (See also Luke 17:26, 27; Matthew 19:4-6; Mark 10:6-9). Divorce was never planned for or intended by God in his purpose for marriage, as Jesus declares in Matthew 19:7, 8.

Later, in Moses' writings, we find a "concession" about divorce made in the giving of his law, as found in Deuteronomy 24:1-4, where the husband is permitted to give a bill of divorcement to the wife if he finds something "unseemly" in her. This bill permits her remarriage to someone else, though if she should be similarly divorced from the second husband the first may not take her again—that would be "an abomination." This "concession" was not commanded or required, but Moses only "suffered" them to do this, "because of the hardness of their hearts" (Matthew 19:8).

The teaching of Jesus relative to marriage and divorce restored the original principle of marriage which was "from the beginning", namely, "one man for one woman", and divorce was henceforth allowed only for the cause of fornication (Matthew 19:8, 9). This single exception of fornication is supported by Matthew 5:32. [The parallel passages in Mark (10:6-9, 11, 12) and Luke (16:18) stipulate what constitutes adultery but do not state the exceptive phrase that would authorize remarriage]. It seems obvious that Jesus' teaching, unlike the law of Moses, allows the same basis for both male and female spouses as far as authorization to divorce is concerned, and does not limit divorce "for fornication" as a choice to the husband only. It probably should be noted here

7

that no one is *commanded* here or elsewhere in the New Testament, to divorce a spouse even in the case of fornication, rather the innocent party is *permitted* to be divorced (and to remarry) if he or she is unable to continue in the first marriage. Surely the better part, on the part of everyone involved, is to forgive and to go ahead and make a success of the first marriage, if it is at all possible. Again, there is always the danger that the "innocent" party may not be so innocent, after all, by having someway caused or contributed to the bad relationship. Only God can assess guilt of this type, but the sensitive Christian should make every effort to be sure that there is no causal guilt on his or her part.

The "twain becoming one flesh" concept that appears frequently in Jesus' teaching and also in the purposes of God "from the beginning" clearly indicate that marriage is for life, and divorce could be allowed only when the "twain" is invaded by a third person and the "one flesh" concept can no longer be maintained. Divorce clearly was never intended. It is a rupture of God's plans, and divorce for trivial reasons is therefore sinful. God expects his people to work out their differences (and there is no reason why they cannot.) People of every age need the realization that "marriage is for keeps." This would help them not to rush into marriage ill-advisedly, but also will prompt them to forget all selfish and petty problems and to really work out family quarrels.

In summary, Jesus taught that marriage was to be breakable only by death, as it had been set up "from the beginning." The one exception which would break the marriage in God's sight and allow remarriage is adultery, or some other act of fornication, committed after the marriage began.

Some commentators make a difference between the teachings of the apostle Paul and what Jesus taught, by emphasizing those things found in Jesus but not referred to by Paul. But it should be observed that Jesus authorized the apostles to speak in his name and by his authority (Matthew 28:18-20; Hebrews 2:3), and thus whatever the apostles taught is in harmony with what Jesus taught. This is really what "inspiration" means. The New Testament is actually the production of the Holy Spirit—if not, then we have no

8

authoritative word of God at all, but if so, then all parts of it speak with equal authority and they agree with each other when rightly interpreted. The Bible need not speak more than once to establish a principle of God's will. If the entire body of scriptures, rightly understood, is not God given and God controlled, how are we to explain the existence and the nature of the Bible itself?

In I Corinthians 7 Paul, though himself unmarried, recommends marriage for Christians who have difficulty with continence, and he presumes that there will be many such Christians. Marriage is honorable and is certainly to be desired over unbridled lust and over those acts it leads to. Married Christians are obligated to minister to the physical needs of their spouses, but may have temporary separations for spiritual purposes (vv. 1-7).

*Single Christians* are to remain single if they can be continent, for in this way they can be more active for the Lord, but, "it is better to marry than to be aflame with passion." (v. 9).

In case *married Christians* prove not to be compatible and simply cannot live together, they may live separately, but in this case they are still married to each other, and cannot divorce and remarry someone else (vv. 10, 11).

Advice to a third group by Paul is for those Christians who are *married to non-Christian spouses* (vv. 12-15). They are to live together if the unbelieving spouse is willing, but if he chooses to "depart" the Christian is "not under bondage in such cases." To be sure the Christian is to take no initiative toward separation, but should do all in his power to keep the marriage going. This passage will be discussed at greater length later.

Paul himself does not give the "exceptive phrase" that fornication is scriptural grounds for divorce, but he doesn't need to since Jesus was positive in this regard. His teaching does parallel that of Jesus however (Romans 7:1-4), in that marriage is clearly to last until death, and sexual union with a third person while one's spouse is alive constitutes adultery. Again in I Corinthians 7:39 Paul notes that the marriage union binds until separated by death. Surely people of our present age need to understand this, and to realize that they trample upon God's will if they divorce only for whatever human law will allow.

Other positive teaching of Paul is found in I Corinthians 6:9, 10, which makes it definite that people guilty of adultery or other types of fornication cannot go to heaven in that condition. An additional significant point in this passage is that people can be fornicators and adulterers, while they are aliens from God's covenant, and BEFORE they become Christians, as was true of those Corinthian brethren. God's law concerning sexual sins, therefore, applies to pagans and people not in covenant relation with him, just the same as it does to Christians. God has many laws that apply to all men alike—stealing, murder, lying, disobedience, fornication, adultery, homosexuality, drunkenness. If not, why not? How can any man say that an adulterous act (or life) for an unbeliever is different from the same thing in a Christian?

One additional point of Paul's teaching on marriage is found in 2 Corinthians 6:14, where he warns us against being unequally-yoked or *mismated* with unbelievers. This is commonly considered as applying to marriage, though to other relationships as well. [Discussion will be given later as to how this relates to the admoniton in 1 Corinthians 7:12-15, where the Christian is to try to maintain his marriage to an unbeliever, if the relation is desired by the latter].

In summary, the New Testament teaching on marriage is that it is a very serious matter, beautiful and wholesome, but subject to potential dangers that can be overwhelming. Marriage is for the entire life, and the only exception is fornication. It has obligations that are very demanding, but rewards and satisfactions that are enriching and happiness producing. Spirituality takes precedence over satisfaction of the flesh, though the latter is good and even blessed when kept in the legitimate framework.

A word should be said here about the relation of God's law on marriage to human civil laws. This writer has often said that "God doesn't pay much attention to what goes on at the local courthouse." By this it is meant that God is not bound by what man does or approves. Human laws can approve a union between two people that God disapproves of and counts to be sin, while man's law can also grant a divorce which God in no way recognizes. People tend to ignore God's will and to assume that if "it's legal", by man's law it is also proper and approved in God's sight.

## STUDY QUESTIONS

### Chapter 2

1. Give the basic requirements of God's "original" marriage law.

2. Comment on the "Mosaic concession". When did it begin and when did it end?

3. Give the major points of Jesus' personal teaching on marriage and divorce.

4. What points are found in Paul's teaching that differ from that of Jesus? What relation do these bodies of teaching have?

5. Distinguish between the instructions Paul gives to each of the three categories in 1 Corinthians 7:8-15.

6. What relation does human civil law have to God's will on marriage and divorce?

# Chapter 3

# RESPONSIBILITY OF THE ALIEN

## The Problem Stated

Does God's marriage law apply only to people in covenant relation with him, such as the Mosaic and Christian covenants, or does it apply to unbelievers and alien sinners as well? Some interpreters of today say that there is no marriage law applicable to non-Christians, thus there are no adulterous unions for them, if human law has approved a marriage. A pagan could thus marry and divorce any number of times without his last marriage being considered adulterous by God, and if he should then become a Christian, his baptism would "sanctify" his last marriage and he would then be eligible to keep the last marriage with divine blessing. Others say that all people are subject to God's marriage regulations regardless of covenantal status, and will be guilty of adultery if they engage in a sexual union while actually married to someone else. Obviously this problem needs to be resolved. If the more liberal interpretation given above is wrong many will end life as unforgiven sinners and will be lost.

## General Arguments

All members of the human race belong to God by creation, and although he has given certain commands to certain individuals or groups on occasion, his moral laws and general principles apply to all. Disobedient people are distinguished from the obedient ones from Adam's day on down. There is a dichotomy in God's mind between "servants" and "sinners" in every age. God is the God of all men, and all owe obligations to him. The wicked in the days of Noah were punished with the flood. The people of Sodom and Gomorrah were punished for fornication (by homo-

12

sexuality) and Jonah preached to Ninevite (non-Jewish) sinners. God in the Christian age is "not wishing that any should perish" but desires that "all should reach repentance" (2 Peter 3:9). Repentance is needed only by the disobedient, but there could be no disobedience if law did not apply to them.

If God's marriage laws and regulations did not apply to aliens none of them would really be married. If no law applied to them they would not be sinners at all, and would need neither salvation nor repentance.

## Specific Passages on Alien Sins

Here we would note references to two groups of alien sins, the one concerning general sins, and the other fornication, or sex-related sins:

*General Sins:*

> Acts 17:31—The times of ignorance God overlooked, but now he commands all men everywhere to repent.
>
> Ephesians 2:1-3—And you he made alive, when you were dead through the trespasses and sins in which you once walked, following the course of this world, following the prince of power of the air, the spirit that is now at work in the sons of disobedience. Among these we all once lived in the passions of our flesh, following the desires of body and mind, and so we were by nature children of wrath, like the rest of mankind.
>
> Ephesians 2:12—remember that you were at that time separated from Christ, alienated from the commonwealth of Israel, and strangers to the covenants of promise, having no hope and without God in the world.
>
> Mark 16:15, 16—And he said to them, "Go into all the world and preach the gospel to the whole creation. He who believes and is baptized will be saved, but he who does not believe will be condemned."
>
> Romans 2:12-16—All who have sinned without [outside of—JDT] the law will also perish without the law, and all who have sinned under the law will be judged by the law. For it is not the hearers of the law who are righteous before God, but the doers of the law who will be justified. When Gentiles who have not the law do by nature what the law requires, they are a law to themselves, even though they do not have the law. They show what the law requires is written on their hearts, while their conscience also bears witness and

13

their conflicting thoughts accuse or perhaps excuse them on that day when, according to my gospel, God judges the secrets of men by Christ Jesus. [Note: This passage shows that NO MAN IS WITHOUT SOME KIND OF LAW IN GOD'S SIGHT.]

1 Peter 4:3-5—Let the time that is past suffice for doing what the Gentiles like to do, living in licentiousness, passions, drunkenness revels, carousing, and lawless idolatry. They are surprised that you do not now join them in the same wild profligacy, and they abuse you; but they will give account to him who is ready to judge the living and the dead.

Acts 2:38—Repent and be baptized every one of you in the name of Jesus Christ for the forgiveness of your sins and you shall receive the gift of the Holy Spirit. For the promise is to you and your children and to all that are afar off . . . . .

Romans 3:9—I have already charged that all men, both Jews and Greeks are under the power of sin . . . . . 23—all have sinned and fall short of the glory of God.

## Fornication or Sins of Sex:

Romans 1:24-32—[Here aliens are condemned for such sins as wickedness, disbelief, impurity, homosexuality, covetousness, malice, envy, murder, and numerous similar sins.]

Colossians 3:5-7—Put to death therefore what is earthly in you: immorality (fornication), impurity, passion, evil desire, and covetousness, which is idolatry. On account of these the wrath of God is coming. In these you once walked, when you lived in them.

1 Corinthians 6:9-11—Do you not know that the unrighteous will not inherit the kingdom of God? Do not be deceived; neither the immoral nor idolaters, nor adulterers, nor homosexuals, nor thieves, nor the greedy, nor drunkards, nor revilers, nor robbers will inherit the kingdom of God. And such were some of you. But you were washed, you were sanctified, you were justified in the name of the Lord Jesus Christ and in the Spirit of our God. [THIS PASSAGE SHOULD SETTLE THE WHOLE QUESTION]

Numerous other passages could be listed to demonstrate that aliens can and do sin and will be held accountable before God for it. They not only sin in general ways but can be guilty of specific sins like fornication (adultery, homosexuality, *etc.*), covetousness, drunkenness, and the like. If an alien can commit adultery (and he can), he must repent of it before he can become a Christian, just like he would have to repent of any other sin.

14

## Objections Considered

Among the objections offered to the idea that the alien in today's world is responsible to God's marriage law and must repent of his adulteries (if any) before he can become a Christian, are offered the following:

1. *One Cannot "Live in Adultery."* A problem here is a claim that adultery is not an illicit sexual union as such, but should be defined as "continually swapping wives (or husbands), and 'getting married' (by man's law) continually." This must surely be an *invented* definition of the word "adultery" for the purposes of this argument, since it is not supportable in the Greek lexicons. Adultery is a "married person having sexual intercourse with a person who is not his divinely approved spouse." The argument goes further by claiming that "one cannot 'live in' anything that is done in single acts, and therefore it is unscriptural to speak of 'living in adultery'.

By way of reply, remember that Colossians 3:5-7 listed numerous former sins of the Colossian Christians, including fornication, and said (v. 7) "In these you once walked, when you lived in them." This one passage repudiates completely the argument that people cannot "live in" adultery. These Colossians, before obeying the gospel, "walked in" and "lived in" these sins, in that they continued the practice of them and constantly lived under the guilt of them. Repeated acts of adultery also qualify exactly here. Ephesians 2:1-3 and also v. 12, all quoted above, say the same thing as to "walking" and "living" in sins, which without doubt include adultery though not specifically mentioned. 1 Corinthians 6:9-11 is a catalog of former sins of some of the Corinthian Christians, mentioning fornication and adultery specifically, and saying "Such were some of you" (i. e., in their former state). The word "were" is the imperfect tense in Greek, which shows that it means "durative or continuous action in past time," thus numerous, repeated actions and continued guilt. In Matthew 19:9, in the famous "exceptive" passage, Jesus said "whoever divorces his wife, except for unchastity, and marries another, commits adultery." The word "commits" is in the present tense (Gnomic present or present of general truth), and therefore, can be considered as "present of habitual action." To be guilty of "living in adultery" is therefore a valid concept.

2. *Baptism removes the sin.* It is true that baptism (of a truly penitent believer) removes the guilt of past sins. But baptism will *not* do a lot of things! It will not make a Jew out of a Gentile, nor a German convert into an American one. It will not change the act of stealing, done before baptism, into an act of righteousness if done afterward. Nor will it make homosexuality to be an approved practice if done by baptized people. Obviously, therefore, if the person with whom one had sex relations was not approved of God before baptism, that same person would not be approved for this purpose AFTER baptism. If a union is adulterous before baptism, that same union will be adulterous after baptism. [In the view of this writer no amount of logic can gainsay this]. Baptism is for the REMISSION OF SINS. These other things it was never purposed to accomplish. It cannot sanctify an unholy sexual union.

If a person is engaged in any unholy practice before baptism—be it dope peddling, liquor merchant, operating a bawdy house, bank-robbing, drunkenness, idolatry, homosexuality or whatever,—*he must give up such* in order to become a Christian, because, even though baptism will clean his past sins, it will not purify such practices and make them to be holy practices.

3. *A Man Should Abide In The Calling in Which He is Called* (1 Corinthians 7:20). This subtle argument claims that "any marriage" of aliens is *honorable* (if it meets human law requirements) and therefore need not be given up in becoming a Christian. Obviously no man could "abide" with approval in any unholy or sinful calling. This latter fact is admitted by some who make this argument, but they counter by stating that *marriage* is "honorable" and therefore, should not be dissolved for the reasons and in the cases being discussed here.

4. *Marriage is honorable, not sinful.* "Let marriage be held in honor among all, and let the marriage bed be undefiled" (Hebrews 13:4). This objection is based upon a subtle mis-defining of marriage. ·The truth is that the Bible uses "marriage" in two senses (as noted in Chapter I)—one

*approved* of God and one *disapproved* by Him. The approved sense is the martial union of two people who are scripturally eligible and no fornication or adultery is involved. The "marriage" that God does not approve is that which human law allows to be legal, but where God's laws do not. Human law, for instance, will allow a "marriage" of two people that God's law counts to be adultery. Passages which illustrate this clearly are:

> Matthew 5:32—Whoever marries a divorced woman commits adultery.

> Romans 7:3—"So then if, while her husband liveth, she be married to another man, she shall be called an adulteress: but if the husband be dead, she is loosed from the law: so that she is no adulteress, though she be married to another man."

> Matthew 19:9—"Whoever divorces his wife, except for unchastity, and marries another, commits adultery." [Obviously the marriage contemplated here is not divinely approved.]

> Mark 6:17—Herod had sent and seized John, and bound him in prison for the sake of Herodias, his brother Philip's wife; because he had married her.

The above passages show that not all "marriages" are God-approved for the simple reason that in his sight they are no more than human-law "contracts for adultery." It is therefore wrong for some interpreters to say that "marriage is honorable" and include adulterous unions in the word "marriage". This is done.

The above claim strangely grants that if an adulterous marriage is contracted AFTER baptism of the parties, then *it must be broken up,* regardless of children or other consequences; but if it was contracted when the parties were aliens, it is "sanctified" by the baptism and becomes an honorable and a blessed union. This means that there would have to be two sets of marriage laws, one for aliens and one for Christians. [What we need here is proof, or evidence that there are two sets of marriage laws, and that adultery before marriage becomes a blessed relationship by baptism.]

In summary on the responsibility of the alien it has been shown that aliens are responsible to God's laws generally, but also specifically, and that they can be guilty of fornication, adultery, homosexuality, in just the same way and by the same conduct as Christians. Numerous passages of scripture were cited to demonstrate these facts. Objections that are commonly made in this area were given and answered. Chief among these is the claim that an illegitimate (adulterous) union entered before Christian baptism becomes sanctified by the baptism. (Nothing is said about what happens in case only one party to the union is baptized). Such interpretation appears far-fetched and one suspects that it is dominated by wishful thinking rather than a serious effort at solid biblical exegesis.

## STUDY QUESTIONS

### Chapter 3

1. State the problems as to whether alien persons are obligated to follow God's law on marriage.

2. Give three passages showing that aliens are amenable to God's laws generally. Three that show they can sin by fornication.

3. Comment on each of the four arguments offered to show that alien "mistakes" in the area of sex will automatically be "washed out" when they become Christians.

4. What arguments can you think of that contradict the arguments of question 3?

# Chapter 4

# THE DEMANDS OF REPENTANCE

The meaning of repentance is a very crucial consideration in our study, so we turn first to definitions found in
lexicons and in the English dictionary:

J. H. Thayer says of *metanoia,* the predominant and
most elevated word translated "repentance"–"to change
one's mind for the better, heartily to amend with abhorrence
of one's past sins."

Bagster's *Analytical Lexicon* gives–"to undergo a change
in frame of mind and feeling, to repent; to make a change of
principle and practice, to reform."

Webster's Seventh *New Collegiate Dictionary* defines,
"to turn from sin and dedicate oneself to the amendment of
one's life."

Next we hear from the New Testament itself: Matthew
21:28, "A man had two sons; and he went to the first and
said, 'Son go to work today in the vineyard. And he
answered, I will not.' but afterward he repented and went."
In this we see that he first willed *not to go,* but when he
repented he *changed his will* and went. So, basically,
repentance is a change of will. But it is more than a change of
mind, it calls for action, for an expression of that change in
new and different conduct. In Acts 26:20 Paul states–
"I . . . declared first to those at Damascus, then at Jerusalem
and throughout all the country of Judea, and also to the
Gentiles, that they should repent and turn to God and
perform deeds worthy of their repentance." This comprehensive statement shows that repentance necessarily calls for
"fruit" or actions which demonstrate the repentance.

Repentance is impossible unless the person reforms his life and does his best to make his wrongs right.

We conclude therefore that repentance requires a change of mind but also a change of will and reformation of life, with reformation and restitution to the extent of one's ability. Anything short of this is not the right attitude, not really repentance.

## Restitution

The heart of the problem concerning divorce and re-marriage revolves to a great extent around what repentance requires, in the matters of change, reformation and restitution. We need to consider this thoroughly:

1) Some hold that God's grace, mercy, and forgiving spirit will cause him to overlook and forgive an adulterous alien marriage because of ignorance and since the parties now have become Christians[3] he will permit the relation to continue with his blessings without any fruit of repentance or change of conduct. In other words, those involved in adulterous union can now as Christians keep right on in that union with God's approval and without changing conduct. An illustration for this argument is offered in God's forgiveness of Paul—"I received mercy because I had acted ignorantly in unbelief" (1 Timothy 1:13). This conclusion however does not take account of the fact that Paul repented. He did not continue on with his same sins after repentance.

Good logic indicates, however, that if the relationship was adulterous prior to baptism, the continued union of the same two people after baptism will be the same way. David and Bathsheba, whose marriage was approved by God, is cited as a case in point to try to show where God simply ignored the past sin and went on from there. This is not true, however, for David and Bathsheba did not marry until after her former husband was dead. Their marriage was therefore not adulterous.

A prominent author also comments on this point:

The last part of our question asks why the sinful relation-

ship of a man with women would not be forgiven and pass
away with all other old things when he obeys the gospel. Of
a truth, all of the man's sins will be forgiven and all of his
past blotted out when he obeys the gospel. If he has had a
thousand sinful relationships with women, all of this will be
forgiven when he repents, but any person who will think
for a moment would know that to repent would mean to
cease to practice such sinful things and to break up all such
sinful relationships. Therefore, if the man is then living in
sin with a woman, he can't continue in that life and repent.
Repentance would mean the giving up of that woman or
those women.[4]

2) It is also argued that sins of ignorance carry a lesser
penalty. People with different native talents have different
responsibilities. The one talent man will be dealt with dif-
ferently than the man of five talents. The logic in this
approach however fails to recognize that *both will be punished* if they fail to repent and do God's will. In the illustration, the man with the least knowledge and abilities gets
punished the most. Another effort to "distinguish between
responsibilities" is the argument that the servant who knew
his master's will and did things wrongly will be punished with
many stripes, while those who knew not but did things
worthy of stripes will be punished with few stripes (Luke
12). Again, this fails to note the conclusion that both commit
sin and both are punished. These are clearly not parallel to
the adulterous marriage problem and fail completely to
justify a continued relationship of adultery. 3) An appeal to
emotions comes with the argument that it is wrong to break
up another marriage, and more especially if there is *love,* and
perhaps children involved. Quotations with emotional appeal
are here illustrated:

> . . . they can destroy this marriage also . . .

> . . . . They purpose to solidify their present marriage and sanctify
> their home to the service of God—have they not actually accom-
> plished what God intended for his marriage law to accomplish?

> They have stemmed the tide of immorality in their own life[5]

> [This admits that it has been an immoral relationship—JDT]

In Ezra 10 we have a case in point of non-approved
marriages and what was done about them:

v. 2–"We have broken faith with our God and have married foreign women from the peoples of the land, but even now there is hope for Israel in spite of this. Therefore, let us make a covenant with our God to put away all these wives and their children, according to the counsel of my Lord and of those who tremble at the commandment of our God; and let it be done according to the law" . . . (11.) Now then make confession to the Lord the God of your fathers, and do his will; separate yourselves from the peoples of the land and from the foreign wives.

In spite of the emotional aspects, this passage makes it clear that God's will is dominant and is what ultimately counts. Families were broken up that had been formed in direct disobedience to God's will. This brings tremendous emotional pressure (especially where relatives or friends of the interpreter are involved) but God's will must be allowed to transcend our personal feelings. Sometimes human civil laws require the break up of a home, even where children are involved, when the father is sent off to prison for life. The carrying out of law requires hardships, even on the part of innocent people, but we all understand this and make the most of it.

4) A strong appeal is seen in the claim that "there are some trespasses that cannot be undone." Murder is given to illustrate a sin which can be repented of but where restitution cannot be made.[6] This even allows for a change of conduct, for the sinner does not plan any more murders, but a change of relationship is not possible, since he can never un-murder the deceased. This is held to be parallel to the penitent adulterer, who can repent (change his mind) and has determined not to enter an adulterous relationship with any new person (change of conduct), but should not be expected to change relationship with the present spouse, which however, began as an adulterous union. What logic!

It is true that a murdered person cannot be restored to life, and there are of course numerous other sins where restitution and retribution could not be made. But the implication that an adulterous union cannot be broken does not follow! If two persons are having an adulterous affair, with or without the blessing of human law, *they can cease* that affair, and in the light of God's will MUST cease it as a part of their repentance of it. You cannot steal and then repent and keep the money. The fruit of sin cannot be kept for personal advantage after repentance, where it is possible to make resti-

22

tution or restoration or to go back to the former situation to any degree.

5) Some people reason that there is a parallel to our problem of "repenting and keeping the present mate" in that 2 Corinthians 6:14 says, "Do not be mismated with unbelievers", and 1 Corinthians 7:39 limits the marriage of a Christian widow to a Christian. In such a case, if a Christian should marry a non-Christian, he would be in disobedience to God and would be guilty of sin. If he chooses to repent, the argument goes, he must put away the non-Christian spouse and therefore must break up the union. Now, since *no one* holds that this type of case should go this far, it is claimed that when the sin of an adulterous union is repented of, it is therefore, not necessary to break up a marital union in this case either.

The reply to the above "logic" calls for the recognition that sometimes one law of God overlaps another in application. In the physical realm, the law of gravity decrees that all objects turned loose in the air will fall to the ground. But if another law intervenes, such as a boy catching a falling baseball, it will not fall all the way to the ground, and the law of gravity is frustrated, in that it does not carry completely through. It is contravened by another law of force which is acting in the same set of circumstances. Likewise, God's law was violated when the mismating occurred, but this, like any wrong, can be repented of.

Now we are ready for the difference between these two cases: In the case of the adulterous union, it is sinful and wrong and must be given up for repentance to occur. In the other case, even though the marriage with the unbeliever is not God's will, *this union is not adulterous,* and, there is another law of God which comes into operation, namely, the law found in 1 Corinthians 7:12-16, which requires that where a Christian is married to an unbeliever and the unbeliever is content to remain in that situation, the Christian is to take no initiative to break up the union. [Some hold that the marriages contemplated in 1 Corinthians 7:12-16 are necessarily those contracted BEFORE baptism into Christ, not AFTER. But this idea is not taught in scripture, nor is it even implied in any way.]

For a summary on repentance, we must determine to let the word of God rise to its authority, above our emotional wishes and preferences. If emotion governs, we can make God's will read any way we want it to. But this is not the road to heaven. Often people must take the difficult road to follow Christ—choose Him above father and mother, over one's wife, or children, even over oneself. Discipleship is oftentimes costly, and God's grace is not cheap. "To obey is better than sacrifice", and if there is no real obedience, there is no faith.

## STUDY QUESTIONS

### Chapter 4

1. Define "repentance", both lexically and from the New Testament.

2. What is restitution? What does it have to do with repentance? How important is it?

3. Outline and discuss each of the four arguments treated, and make clear why some persons feel that the newly baptized Christian can keep on living with his spouse, even though scriptural teachings would not justify the union.

4. Give replies to the arguments of question 3.

# Chapter 5

# PRINCIPLES OF INTERPRETATION

An understanding of how the will of God is communicated to man is all essential at this point in our study. Where and how do we find it, through what avenues is the revelation expected to come, and what assurance do we have that we can be certain and definite that we have the will of God rather than something we only imagine to be the will of God?

Traditionally the canonical scriptures have had acceptance as the revelation of God's will. There have been claims about more or less "direct revelations" to individuals. Within the past one hundred and fifty years philosophy has advanced notions about *subjective* avenues through which truth may come to the individual, and some theologies, particularly existentialism, have become addicted to this idea. Since subjectivities have no way of testing themselves or proving that they are no more than imagination or wishful thinking, we have more certainty if we limit ourselves to the Bible, and in the Christian age to the New Testament. These Christian scriptures have withstood the test of time and have within themselves evidences of supernatural influence in their production. They clearly declare the will of Jesus Christ and the revelation given through his apostles, so our concern will be to go "To the teaching and to the testimony" (Isaiah 8:20).

Proper interpretation of scripture calls for a careful exegesis ("leading out" of the meaning) of the text of the original language. This must obviously be done by trained scholars, of which most religious groups have some. Differences between scholars can be worked out, unless some (and scholars are also human) insist on doing *eisegesis* (reading into the passage) meanings about which they have pre-commitments. Admittedly denominational prejudices and preferences have entered into Biblical interpretation, but there is no justification for this. The ideal, therefore, is to let the Bible alone be our authority in learning God's will, and when it speaks, lay our personal thinking aside and "let the chips fall where they may."

There is a school of thought known to some as "the restoration movement" whose members accept Christ and the scriptures as his word, and hold as a basic tenet that "scripturalness" is the prime criterion for determining God's will on any matter. The scriptures must be correctly interpreted, to be sure, and these thinkers accept the usual scholarly techniques and methods in so far as they are objectively used and applied.[7]

The basic thinking of this group, however, holds to the idea of the scripture interpreting itself, where such is possible, and great care is taken to avoid what might be termed as mere human authority or man's wisdom. If an idea cannot be clearly supported by the scriptures it is invalid as far as binding obligation is concerned. This means that subjectivisms, private revelations, and direct operations of the Holy Spirit furnishing objective messages to man today are not counted as worthy of consideration. The Bible itself can be understood by the ordinary man without supernatural help, since it is inspired and says in human language exactly what God wants man to know. It does not take premonitions, special illumination, hunches, or a super interpreter specially ordained, but was planned to be known through a serious application of the intellect and reason of the normal man.

### Jesus and Paul

In interpretation we must not array Paul's teaching on divorce and remarriage against that of Jesus. Hebrews 1:1 observes that God's will in this age comes to man "through his Son," and Hebrews 2:3 notes that the revelation was "declared at first by the Lord," and it was then "attested to us by those who heard him." This means that the apostles were but agents of Christ in their teaching, and that what they taught is to be understood as his teaching. To be sure there are a few points about which some people make a difference between Jesus and Paul, but we insist that this is unjustified. Possible points of difference will be discussed

26

at proper places later in this study, and we trust that it will be shown that there is no disagreement.

The New Testament itself argues against human, uninspired doctrine and warns against going outside of scripture for religious authority:

Matthew 15:8, 9—This people honoreth me with their lips, but their heart is far from me; in vain do they worship me, teaching as doctrine the precepts of men.

2 John 9—Anyone who goes ahead and does not abide in the doctrine of Christ does not have God; he who abides in the doctrine has both the Father and the Son.

Galatians 1:6-8—I am astonished that you are so quickly deserting him who called you in the grace of Christ and turning to a different gospel—not that there is another gospel, but there are some who trouble you and want to pervert the gospel of Christ. But even if we, or an angel from heaven, should preach to you a gospel contrary to that which we preached to you, let him be accursed.

Romans 16:17— . . . take note of those who create dissensions and difficulties, in opposition to the doctrine which you have been taught; avoid them.

2 Thessalonians 3:6—Now we command you, brethren, in the name of our Lord Jesus Christ, that you keep away from any brother who is living in idleness and not in accord with the tradition that you received from us.

Titus 1:13, 14— . . . rebuke them sharply, that they may be sound in the faith, instead of giving heed to Jewish myths or to commands of men who reject the truth.

Romans 10:17—So faith comes from what is heard, and what is heard comes by the preaching of Christ.

I Corinthians 4:6— . . . that you may learn to live according to scripture.

From the above passages the conclusion comes with force that doctrinal authority in Christianity comes only from the inspired New Testament. However human teachings may enlighten, they of themselves do not establish authority.

## AUTHORITY IN EARLY CHURCH HISTORY?

A significant problem for knowing God's will about divorce and remarriage is the impact which the attitudes and actions of the early church (*after* the inspired scriptures were completed) should have upon our knowledge today about God's definite will. Clearly they can aid our understanding of some New Testament teachings, but some seem to conclude that we can learn positively about God's will on the divorce and remarriage problem from early Christian writings alone, since they hold that the New Testament itself does not give a full and positive knowledge on this problem.[8] The claim needs careful investigation.

Specifically, the New Testament itself ("primary legislation"—in their terminology) does not make it clear whether an adulterous mate can be kept after one becomes a Christian, but the writings of early uninspired Christians ("secondary legislation") show historically what the attitude of the early church was toward the problem, and therefore these writings in and of themselves furnish positive and conclusive knowledge that such a mate can be retained with divine approval. This "secondary legislation" is actually the *absence* of any comment about the problem. It is held that since we are not given details showing that such mates had to be put away, this lack of treatment in the early Christian literature proves positively that it was an unimportant question, and that a new Christian, who had previously been living in adultery, could now maintain his existing marital union with God's blessing. Note the following quotations, given to prove this point:

> The secondary legislation is revealed in the New Testament. While not expressed in explicit terms, it is none-the-less clearly expressed in implicit terms. The implications concerning the secondary legislation are just as emphatic as the explicit teachings are concerning the primary legislation.[9]

Just how such strong authorization can be "only implicit," and yet be as clear and emphatic as the explicit teachings of the New Testament on this subject, escapes the present writer. Further, how could anything be so clear and positive when it is based completely on silence —on the absence of any comment about the subject in extant Christian literature?

One writing of today speaks of this "non-testimony" as "the divine application" of the divorce law as it was "applied" in the first centuries.[10] It says further, the "writings of an era reflect the thinking of that era,"[11] (as though it does so with infallible finality), and the author then draws the assumption that "interpreters of history are able to determine accurately the attitudes, customs, and practice of a people at a given time in history."[12]

Several things may be wrong with the above conclusions:

*First,* there is only a small amount of early Christian literature extant today, as compared with what once existed. To base Christian doctrine on whether a person is living in sin, on such a small amount of the literature (even if it were infallibly authoritative to begin with) would be highly questionable.

*Second,* the "divorce law" conclusion derived on the basis of what early Christian literature indicates, is actually based on *what is not found* in these writings. This is an "argument from silence," and in truth anything could be proved by what is NOT said. (For example, liberal scholars once argued that Moses could not have written the Pentateuch, for "Semitic alphabetic writing did not exist in his day." The truth was that they had not yet found any such writing at that time and were only arguing from silence. Since then much of such writings has been found and the argument is no longer made.) When anyone argues anything from what is *not* said, he is free to imagine whatever he wishes and claim its truth, without fear of being refuted. We must realize that to argue early church understandings from what is not said in the historical documents has no logical validity.

As a matter of fact, early Christian writings do NOT say anything about several subjects. We must not assume that the early church approved continuance of the numerous sinful practices (1 Corinthians 6:9-11. e. g.) engaged in by baptized persons, if the early Christian literature does not happen to specifically warn Christians to discontinue them. It logically follows that repentance, a requirement for becoming a Christian, and which by definition requires the giving up of such sins as one has been guilty of, takes care of the matter of the revelation to later ages of what God requires, without needing specific instances of the understanding of the early church. This is just as true of one's *living in an adulterous union* as it is of other sins. The explicit (primary legislation) teaching of the New Testament is adequate within itself when fully interpreted and understood. The "secondary legislation" idea is valid only for confirmation and perhaps clarification in knowing God's will. When a man repents he quits practicing his sins!

*Third,* only the Bible is God's inspired word, infallible and inerrant, for the establishment of firm doctrine. The restoration movement is committed to restoring New Testament Christianity, based upon the canonical scriptures, not that of the uninspired literature of the second (or later) Christian centuries. Whatever truth we accept must ultimately be known to be taught in the New Testament, though the early literature is often helpful.

*Fourth,* the early Christian writers disagreed with each other. Which ones among them reflect the proper understanding for us to follow?

*Fifth,* at what point in history does the exclusive "authority bearing" of the Christian writers cease, or does it continue right on down into our own age?

*Sixth,* one could prove several unacceptable doctrines to be "scriptural" if he assumed that the uninspired early Christian authors had absolutely right understanding about things. Some of them sanctioned doctrines which are contrary to the New Testament, such as premillennialism, monarchial bishops and diocesan authority, continuing charismatic claims, infant baptism, and later a pope. Even in the days of the New Testament itself some persons held to unsound ideas and practices—Diotrephes, the Nicolaitanes, and the Galatian Judaizers. God was displeased with these. We must not assume that because a group of uninspired people (of any size) had a certain understanding about God's will that it was therefore correct. That is why an inspired scripture was needed in the first place, to guarantee correctness in doctrine. Only it can inform us with certainty about what it takes to please God. If the New Testament does not authorize a principle or a teaching or an action, it is not authorized! To determine from silence the attitude of the early church, and bind that upon oneself today, is to be governed by questionable authority.

30

We are surely limited to the New Testament for our rule of faith and practice. Human authority cannot be acceptable. Any sin repented of had to be given up completely, by definition of the word. If a sin or a sinful relationship was not fully repented of, that person could not truly be baptized into Christ.

Church history does give extremely valuable knowledge that may confirm New Testament teaching or throw light on a passage, and thus give us today a further assurance as to correct interpretation, but such must be accepted only as confirmatory of New Testament teaching. Church history furnishes strong confirmation to the principle of using only a cappella music in the public worship of the church. The literature and the New Testament are in harmony on this point.

What we question in this chapter is the claim that "since canonical scripture does not give the total needed revelation on what alien adulterers should do when they come into the church," *we have to go outside of God's word* to learn what he wishes us to know about his will on this point. We question also that the answer is to be found only in the absence of explicit information! In the case of using a cappella music in worship, on the other hand, the New Testament itself furnishes adequate revelation, and when we look at early church history, we find it fully confirmed. Church history is very valuable, therefore, but not in the way it has been used in this effort to make a case for "sanctifying" adultery.

# STUDY QUESTIONS

## Chapter 5

1. Define "subjective" revelations.

2. Describe the certainty and definiteness one can have with the word revelation of the Bible.

3. Comment on exegesis and the need for scholarly precision.

4. What is the "restoration movement"? What does it hold as to how to know God's will.

5. Give New Testament statements regarding its own as versus other teachings.

6. Give the claim of some who wish to derive valid teaching on our problem from church history over and above scripture.

7. List some reasons why only the New Testament is authoritative for us today.

# Chapter 6

# DO CONSEQUENCES NEGATE SIN?

The problem involved in the question discussed in this chapter is whether or not certain heavy consequences of particular sins committed by humans are so bad that God would therefore mitigate the penalties, and some have concluded that he will make special allowances for certain circumstances—say, where innocent children might have to share in the burden of the punishment. This, of course, is the sort of argument that all sinners make about hell—"It is too much punishment" for the sort of sin that the individual sinner is guilty of. One trouble with this sort of thinking is that sinners themselves cannot fairly evaluate how much punishment certain sins should be due. A jury of bank robbers would not be chosen nor would they be expected to fairly assess punishment for another bank robber on trial. Sinners have an overpowering sympathy for other sinners because we are emotionally involved, and this prevents us from being fair judges. All of us are sinners, and should therefore be careful about forming conclusions about the rightful consequences of sins, and we must bring ourselves to realize that what God has revealed in his word is the only thing that we can go by. We must not rationalize consequences away because we do not like them or because they are not emotionally appealing.

Most people are aware that others are often dominated by emotions and thereby make mistakes. A common example is a young girl who falls in love with an unworthy young man. Her parents recognize the true state of affairs and try to warn her, but because she has "already fallen" she cannot rise to logic, and her will is completely dominated by her emotions. She decides her parents do not know, or are not fair. But later, she slowly realizes that she has made a grievous mistake, and then it is too late. Emotion alone cannot be the basis of good judgment.

Others of us run the risk of being dominated by emotions rather than good sound logic in questions of divorce and remarriage, because we have good friends or close relatives who are already mixed up in a questionable situation, and so we seek out a Bible interpreter who will say to us "favorable words." Once the present writer was asked to say a wedding ceremony, but investigation indicated the couple were not scripturally eligible to marry each other. Upon being refused, they went to another preacher, who complied with their request and was then declared by them to be "one of the world's smartest preachers."

"Cold turkey truth" is what we are going to need when we stand before the judgment bar of God. The preacher who insists on giving us that, is really the one who loves us most. Because of love or any other emotional involvement we cannot afford to dodge factual truth, nor fail to repent genuinely and completely of our sins. Ignorance is no justification for sin, as we are all well aware.

### The Claims

Claims that are used in arguing for the privilege of keeping the most recent spouse of one or more wrong unions when aliens desire to become Christians include:

1) LOVE. A happy home has now developed and a psychologically good marriage has been achieved. This should not be broken up (more especially if there are children of this union). Good marriages where love truly exists are hard to come by, and it surely must be wrong interpretation to cancel out a happy marriage because of a sin of ignorance, so the reasoning goes.

2) THE CHILDREN. In this claim we find a great emotional appeal and tug at our heartstrings. To require a home to be broken up and small children be deprived of one of their parents and have to suffer the consequences for the sins of someone else is too much. A good God would not punish children in this way. There has to be some way to forgive and still let the family remain together.

3) CELIBACY followed for spiritual purposes is freighted

with too many problems to be a justifiable answer. For a mistake made in ignorance, this is too much punishment to visit upon a person. Life is too long, and the sex-drive is too strong, to expect anyone to follow this demand. It wouldn't be fair.

## Replies to the Claims

We shall reply to each of the above basic claims by their same numbers:

1) LOVE. We remind our readers that an adulterous union between a man and a woman is not a "marriage" in God's sight, however happy or pleasant it might be. According to Matthew 19:9 they "are committing adultery" (Gnomic present tense—repeated action). In no way can this be acceptable to God. That aliens *can and do* commit adultery is clear from 1 Corinthians 6:9-11; and Colossians 3:5 says the same thing of fornication, of which adultery is one expression.

To cease an adulterous union therefore is not the same as ceasing a marriage. It is rather the demand of repentance upon the ones who have been practicing it.

The *consequences* of ceasing a marital union that is a sinful relationship cannot be taken into account, even though the union, in human judgment, is happy and beautiful. Human judgment must defer to the scriptures.

2) THE CHILDREN. As indicated, this has the highest emotional appeal of all the arguments. Certainly no one in his right mind would wish suffering or deprivation to come to children, but we also realize that emotion must not overcome logic. Whatever is finally accepted as truth must be logically sound, and then the proper emotions will flow out of that truth.

In Ezra 10:1-4 and v. 11, it is clear that God was displeased with his people marrying "foreign wives" in contradiction to his law, and that in order to be well-pleasing unto him the wives and children had to be given up. (Note again the text of this passage from chapter 4). The Jews had sinned, and their repentance demanded that the sin be undone as far

35

as possible—even to children (perhaps of happy homes) being deprived of a father. No amount of emotion can gainsay this logic. Our trouble is in not realizing how bad sin is. Like the people of the world, we all tend to want to think that sin isn't very bad. But it is bad enough to send people to hell for eternity!

Those who argue that alien adulterers can keep their present spouse when they become Christians admit that if a person has already been baptized and is therefore a child of God BEFORE he gets involved in adultery, and if he then decides to repent and straighten up his life with God HE HAS TO GIVE UP HIS WIFE AND CHILDREN (if any), of the adulterous union. In this case they do not make all the emotional claims about "destroying the marriage" or "doing injustice to the children." It is clearly understood by all of us that the Christian's repentance requires the putting away of the relationship. This illustration shows, then, that these interpreters make a radical difference between alien adulterers and Christian adulterers. They are arguing, in effect, that God has *two laws*—one for aliens and one for Christians. Repentance thus means two different things! For the Christian there is no argument about his having to put away his partner in sin. But for the alien, he can keep her if he wants to! The present writer sees no logic or sound reasoning whatever in this. In scripture we do not find *two laws of marriage,* nor *two meanings of repentance.*

Further, in the case of polygamous marriages, perhaps a few missionaries have refused to face up to scripture, but most Christian teachers (even denominational ones) understand that polygamy has to stop, for people to be good Christians. Given time, "Christian" teaching (by all groups) does away with polygamy in cultures where it has been practiced. Natives see this, under proper teaching, and accept reformation of practice in this as well as in the other demands that repentance and right living make. In this case also, no emotional claim is made about the children. They can be cared for and need not be mistreated. In fact, *the only demand of repentance with respect to adultery is that the persons cease cohabitation,* because that is what adultery is! They do not have to make any other changes, which are frequently assumed to have to go with repentance from adultery.

Surely no one would defend concubinage; or, commune marriages, where many men and many women live together, each cohabiting with whomever he pleases. To become Christians such sins must be given up, and if children should get hurt, we all still say that the repentance must be complete. As another illustration, we do not get excited about "harm done to children" if our state law requires a father to be sent to the penitentiary for life. We understand this, that certain wrongdoing must be punished. There is no escape from relatives and friends being hurt when any person does wrong. This is life.

3) CELIBACY for spiritual ends. It is quite easy for us to reason that it is too much punishment for a messed-up life to require a permanent celibacy for spiritual ends. Apparently some Bible interpreters feel an obligation to guarantee a happy sex life to all, especially if the person is a close relative or friend. We do not gainsay him having such feelings and wishes, but we do gainsay letting them motivate his thinking and ruining his logic in the face of God's word which clearly requires such celibacy, of some persons in some situations.

For instance, in Matthew 5:31, 32 we learn that a wife who is *unjustly* "put away" will be caused to become an adulteress (this assumes that she will unite with someone else). If she does not enter a new relationship, she is condemned to permanent celibacy (Unless of course her husband later commits adultery). She therefore is at his mercy. Our human reasoning would say that this is not fair to her, to be denied any kind of sex relationship for all of her natural life when *she* hasn't done anything wrong at all. This does seem hard and unfair in our judgment, but it is God's law, and there is no question about the right understanding of it.

1 Corinthians 7:10, 11 gives the same teaching—if two Christians separate (and they may if they cannot live together) they must remain unmarried (to any other person). This, then, requires celibacy for life (unless there is reconciliation or one breaks over) and it is a clear, positive requirement of God's law. So, without question, God does require celibacy of some people in some circumstances! It should not seem strange, therefore, that some adulterers who have messed up their lives so much that permanent celibacy should be the

only course open to them for salvation. When Jesus' disciples thought on spiritual celibacy, some of them reasoned that it was all so complicated that it might be best not to marry at all (Matthew 19:10-12), but the Lord pointed out that for some people, being a spiritual eunuch would be the desirable thing to do. Certainly it would be a small concession to make in one's life if it were understood to be necessary to keep one from hell. When the stakes are this high, this is not a big problem!

## Summary

- *Emotion* is legitimate when it flows out of a clear and logical understanding of God's truth. It alone is not a basis for sound judgment.
- *Ignorance* is no excuse for violation of human law, nor God's law. It justifies neither crime nor sin. It does not cancel punishment.
- Appeals on behalf of *"deprived children"* never justify a failure to repent.
- Permanent *celibacy*, if required, is not as bad as hell. In some situations it is indeed required.
- The *consequences* of sin *do not negate the sin* nor the need for genuine repentance.

## STUDY QUESTIONS

### Chapter 6

1. How do you feel about sinners deciding how much punishment sin should have?

2. What relation should reason and emotion have as we make our important decisions?

3. Why is the divorce and remarriage problem often dominated by emotion?

4. Give the claims made for maintaining the wrong type of marriage because of bad consequences?

5. What replies are offered to the claims of question 4?

6. Evaluate the summary statements given at the close of the chapter.

# Chapter 7

# BAPTISM AND THE ALIEN ADULTERER-1

The problem we face in this chapter as we examine what happens when an alien adulterer is baptized, is not so much the discussion and evaluation of new arguments, but one of recapitulation and more precise and detailed examination and evaluation of some that have already been considered. This approach will help overcome the present writer's own limitations in the organization and presentation of materials, and is planned, by repetition and drill, to emphasize and further clarify a crucial matter that has been in extreme confusion and has spiritual life and death as its stakes.

We first, then, would review and comment further on some crucial definitions:

1. *Fornication* (Greek *porneia*) is an illicit sexual relationship. If there is no sexual union, there is no fornication. Some have defined the word as "getting married recklessly and frequently" (or similar terminology), and thus when a man finally gets a woman he can be satisfied with, he keeps her and quits his "much marrying"—thereby quitting his "fornication," and thus can be said to have repented of it. Patently this "invented" meaning of the word must have been conjured up to justify someone keeping a preferred mate. It has no relation whatever to the true meaning of the word, as is noted from the lexicons in Chapter I, or as can be found in other recognized authorities. No scholar of repute would ever come up with such a definition.

*Fornication* is a generic term and has the meaning of any kind of *sexual expression* between persons other than by a man and a woman united in scriptural marriage.

A few people have the impression that *fornication* and

*adultery* are parallel terms, fornication being limited to illicit sexual activity BEFORE marriage, and adultery the same thing DURING marriage. This concept thus would have numerous fornicators in all the churches, and would allow any man who wishes to put away his wife scripturally if he learned that she had committed a sexual indiscretion when she was young, though she is now faithful as a wife. For the church to "withdraw fellowship" from fornicators with this definition would mean that only pre-marital virgins, male and female, could be Christians, even though some other person had been forgiven by God for this sin committed when in his youth. It should be easy to see why such a definition is preposterous even without using lexical authorities.

2. *Adultery* (Greek—*moichaeia*) is fornication between two persons where one or both of them is scripturally married to someone else.

3. *Marriage*—This term was adequately defined in Chapter I, and here we would accent the fact that there are two biblical meanings:
1) a "scriptural" union of eligible persons, thus one approved by God.
2) an unscriptural, adulterous union (where at least one of the parties is scripturally married to someone else). This kind of marriage is sometimes approved by human civil law, though not by God's law.

To further sharpen the idea that the word "marriage" is used in these two different senses, and is often applied in the wrong sense to try to sanctify an adulterous union, we quote here from a well-known writer on this topic:

Matt. 19:9—says plainly that such a marriage is a sinful act; therefore, of course, it is not an approved act. But he says it is *a marriage!* Yes, but it is a marriage by an *unmarriageable person.* A man may deed you a piece of property, and in form and verbiage the deed may be correct, but if it turns out that the man did not own the property, even though he thought he did, you will certainly never hold it. Then in *sound* we would have another contradiction of terms. He sold you the property, yet he did not sell it to you. You bought the property, yet you did not buy it. The answer is plain, the deal *was a deal,* but it was not a legal deal and will not stand up in the eyes of the law.

Take another illustration: A man, who has a wife and children in Tennessee pretends to be and is received as a single or unmarried man. He courts a woman and *marries* her. Yes, *marries* her. Then, this deceived woman and the people from Texas learn that the man has a wife in Tennessee from whom he was not even divorced. He married the woman, by the authority of the law of the state, had a license, and a proper ceremony. But he is not married in the sight of the law! He is a bigamist. He was not in a marriageable status when he married. Cannot our brother see from this how one can be married and yet not be married? Let us hope so, his error here is vicious. [13]

The scriptures themselves speak of such unscriptural unions as "marriages" in Matthew 5:32, 19:9; Mark 6:17 and Romans 7:3. An adulterous union of alien persons is thus a "marriage" in our No. 2 meaning, but not in the No. 1 approved sense.

The serious problem about this for our discussion in this book is that some interpreters give to a No. 2 situation a No. 1 definition, and thus seek to clothe the illicit, yet adulterous union, with divine blessing, since "marriage" is honorable!

Please also note that when a much-married alien adulterer takes on a new wife it is never a "marriage" in the No. 1, divinely approved sense, but as far as God is concerned, it is only "a contract for adultery." If repentance should later cause such a union to dissolve it is *not* the "breaking up of a holy marriage."

The mis-application, therefore, of Hebrews 13:4—"Let the marriage be held in honor among all" to indicate that it can include an alien adulterous union, and that Christians should honor such a relationship is a serious breach of the interpreter's art. Indeed, the rest of the verse should also be considered—"let the marriage bed be undefiled; for God will judge the immoral (fornicators) and adulterous!" The last part of the verse is rarely quoted in this connection.

### The Alien Obligation

No man has ever been without law before God! Starting in the garden of Eden man had obligations to God, and knew about them. Sin entered when man failed to live up to them. A law of marriage was among the first given. Cain violated his obligations and was a sinner and condemned. Romans 1:20ff. shows that man has always had opportunity to adequately know God enough to seek out his specific will, and to live well-pleasing before him.

During the Mosaic period the Gentiles were not in the Mosaic covenant and, as Ephesians 2:12 states, "remember that you were at that time separatęd from Christ, alienated from the commonwealth of Israel, and strangers to the covenants of promise, having no hope and without God in the world."

But, being "without God" and "having no hope" requires that they be guilty as sinners. What law did they violate if they were not amenable to Moses' law? The answer is found in Romans 2:12-14:

> "All who have sinned without (outside of) the law will also perish without the law, and all who have sinned under the law will be judged by the law" ...[14] "When Gentiles who do not have the law do by nature what the law requires, they are a law to themselves, even though they do not have the law."

Obviously Gentiles sin by violating *their own law*— i. e., by violating whatever divine laws that filtered down to them through tradition, by whatever moral laws they figured out for themselves and adopted, and by violating their own consciences. Any one of these violations is a sin before God. Thus, when Romans 3:9 says, "both Jews and Greeks are under the power of sin," and Romans 3:23 says, "all have sinned and fallen short of the glory of God," there is no question but that all non-Mosaic-covenant peoples sinned in all kinds of ways just the same as the Jews sinned. This would obviously include violating God's will in sexual and marriage problems.

Romans 8:7 has been cited to prove that the alien is not amenable to God's law—"For the mind set on the flesh is hostile to God; it does not submit to God's law, indeed it cannot; and those who are in the flesh cannot please God." If this passages proves this point surely something is wrong. If they were not amenable to God's will, there would be no hostility to God. The reason they do not submit and are not pleasing is that they are "the mind set on the flesh" type of person. If they will repent and set their minds on things of the Spirit, the picture will be the opposite. To say they *cannot* submit to God's law, and to understand that this is final and they have no chance whatever, is to fail to understand both this passage and the rest of the Bible. People can change their mind-set.

In Jesus' teaching in Matthew 19:4-9 he makes reference to the original marriage law; to "the Mosaic concession"; and then to the return to the original expectation—with the "exceptive phrase" of divorce for fornication:

> He answered, "Have you not read that he who made them from the beginning made them male and female, and said, "For this reason a man shall leave his father and mother and be joined to his wife, and the two shall become one"? So they are no longer two but one. What therefore God has joined together, let no man put asunder." They said to him, "Why then did Moses command one to give a certificate of divorce, and to put her away?" He said to them, "For your hardness of heart Moses allowed you to divorce your wives, but from the beginning it was not so. And I say to you: whoever divorces his wife except for unchastity, and marries another, commits adultery."

Note the repeated expression, "from the beginning," which takes us back to the garden of Eden when the original law was given. It was to apply to all Adam's descendants—thus no man has been without a marriage law. The Mosaic concession of divorce for minor reasons by the husband, was not a part of the original law, nor is it of the Christian law. (Details of the concession may be noted in Deuteronomy 24:1-4).

In Jesus' "I say unto you" he with full authority repudiated the Mosaic program and restored the original, with only the change of a privilege of divorce being allowed to the innocent party if adultery occurs. This Christian teaching is applicable to all humanity during the Christian age, because now there is no longer Jew and Greek—we are all one in responsibility. There is only one covenant applicable and one hope open for all humanity—through Christ—and so the gospel is preached to every creature. An understanding of God's overall scheme of redemption shows that Christ as Saviour and his New Testament are the one and only way of salvation today—and it is for every human.

Some claim, however, that God's *marriage law* today is only for the church, but they do not explain why aliens have to keep other laws of God that are valid in this dispensation, while being exempt from its laws of marriage. Further, they do not offer scriptural justification for "two laws of marriage" of any kind—one for Christians and another for aliens. Man is a responsible moral being with freedom of choice. There can be no such thing as a "free-wheeling" human with no law to answer to. The approval of civil law is no justification for violation of God's moral laws. Civil law sometimes allows such things as polygamy, slavery, idolatry and covetousness. To claim justification for alien adultery "because civil law authorized it" does not prove anything.

## STUDY QUESTIONS

### Chapter 7

1. Discuss the meaning of fornication in the light of the ideas some have about it.

2. Exactly what is adultery?

3. Give two differing meanings for "marriage" and quote biblical verses illustrating each.

4. Comment on the illustrations quoted in Note 13.

5. How did Gentiles sin (what law did they violate)?

6. Why do some try to show that Gentiles are not under God's marriage law?

7. Prove that all men today are amenable to Christ's laws.

# Chapter 8

# BAPTISM AND THE ALIEN ADULTERER-2

### Living in Adultery

The charge is made that the term "living in adultery" is an illogical concept, inasmuch as adultery is done *in single acts*. The validity of the terminology and the idea it seeks to communicate are well defended, however:

> The critic thinks that the expression "living in adultery" is incorrect, and that is not surprising since he contends that such a relationship or state of life is not wrong. He asks why we do not speak of people's living in lying or living in theft. We do, except that we use correct English in expressing the thought. The exact meaning is expressed by the words *liar* and *thief*. We have the precise equivalent of that expression in the New Testament. Paul says that a woman who is *married* (note the word, brother) to another man "while her husband liveth," "shall be called an adulteress." Our correspondent would say, "You are wrong, Paul, she is not an adulteress, she is *married*!" An adulteress is one who commits adultery; not one who did, at one time, commit this sin but is *guilty,* therefore, in a state of guilt. The man at Corinth (1 Cor. 5) gives us another case. Paul said *there is fornication* among you, which means there is fornication *practiced* among you; a continued state of fornication. The case of Herod is proof of the point, also.[14]

Another argument made for the same purpose concerns the tense of the Greek verb (*moichatai*). In Matthew 19:9, its translation is "commits adultery," but the literal meaning of the Greek tense (Gnomic present) indicates habitual or repeated activity.[15] One recent writer has said:

> Another superficial interpretation is our Doctrine of Living in Adultery. This phrase itself is not in the Bible. While one

46

might think we would use it in reference to some lustful scoundrel with no self-control, it is used rather to refer to even godly Christian husbands and wives who are supposedly still "half married" to the first mate. The argument is all based upon the tense of a Greek verb. It is argued that since "commits adultery" is in the present tense it indicates a continuous relationship of adultery.

Actually the present tense isn't so limited:

The fundamental significance of the present tense is the idea of progress. It is the linear tense. This is not, however, its exclusive significance. It is a mistake to suppose "that the durative meaning monopolizes the present stem . . . since there is no aorist tense for the present time. The present time, as used in the indicative, must do service for both linear and punctiliar action." (Dana and Mantey, *A Manual Grammar of the Greek New Testament*, pp. 181-182).

Our Living in Adultery doctrine, then, isn't nearly so ironclad as has been thundered from the pulpits.[16]

In reply to the above argument we point out that this author has singled out a very *unusual* instance, and he would leave the impression that the unusual aspect is usual enough to be applicable to Matthew 19:9. A few lines further, Dana and Mantey say,

The *progressive force* of the present tense should *always be considered as primary,* especially with reference to the potential moods, which in the nature of the case do not need any "present punctiliar" tense. (Italics mine—JDT)

Then further, in illustrating and discussing this rare use of the present, Dana and Mantey quote from Ernest DeWitt Burton's grammar concerning an "aoristic present":

*"This use is a distinct departure from the prevailing use* of the present tense to denote action in progress . . . There being in the indicative no tense which represents an event as a single fact without at the same time assigning it either to the past or the future, the present is used for those instances *(rare as compared with the cases of the Progressive Present)* in which an action of present time is conceived of without reference to its progress" (Br 9). The student would do well to note in this observation of Burton's a vivid foregleam of the basal significance of the aorist tense. (Italics mine—JDT)

We see therefore the conclusion of these recognized grammarians that the normal and primary use of the present tense is progressive, durative and continuous. Only rarely does it refer to point action, and then only when the context demands it. To say that the word in our context meant only a "one time" action, since Jesus said that "the man who divorces his wife, except for fornication, and marries another commits adultery," is preposterous. He repeatedly does it (Gnomic present of customary or repeated action). He *lives in adultery* with the new partner.

### Herod and David

It is well known that King Herod took his brother Phillip's wife and married her. In this he sinned two ways, by entering an incestuous relationship with a near relative, and also by taking another man's wife in adultery. John the Baptist by inspiration, said to Herod, "It is not lawful for you to have your brother's wife" (Mark 6:17). It is obvious that if Herod had been willing to begin living acceptably before God he would have had to "cease the relationship." [It has been claimed that Herod's only sin in this was the incest, but not the adultery. But one only has to check the word "adultery" and its cognates in a complete concordance to find that it was a common sin in Old Testament days, and that God was highly displeased with it.] Why people of today will argue that an adulterous union can in some way come to have God's blessing without repentance of the activity is beyond the comprehension of this writer.

David's marriage to Bathsheba has also been suggested as an unholy relationship that had God's blessing, but this is done without careful thinking. It is true that they once committed adultery, but this was repented of. At the time of their marriage Bathsheba was a widow. So there is no idea of God sanctioning or even tolerating a continuous adulterous relationship.

### Abiding in Your Calling

In 1 Corinthians 7:20 we read, "Every one should remain in the state in which he was called." The context makes clear that this means *temporal* relationships—the Jew should not

48

want to become a Gentile, the slave should be coi
that status for he is really a freedman in the Lord, e
Christian who is married to an unbeliever should n
to be loosed from that relation, and those in other te̱ ____
and earthly unions should make the most of their situations
for Christ. The problem of this passage is the idea held by
some that if you are involved in an adulterous marriage, and
wish to obey the gospel, you "should still abide in that
particular marriage," which meaning was never intended by
Paul. In no way is this passage meant to sanction and bless
adultery or any other sinful relationship. It applies only to
earthly and "non-spiritual" relations where sin is not involved.
Those who use it wrongly in the divorce problem say that
one is to *remain in* an alien-begun adulterous union, and
which somehow they hope will be sanctified and made
blessed by their baptism, so that the same union can continue.

Obviously, when people repent and are baptized they
must give up their homosexuality, their polygamy, their
idolatry, and all other sinful attitudes and practices which
God's word labels as sinful, regardless of whether their own
culture approves or allows the practice. Oftentimes what
human law or human culture approves is different from what
God approves. We need to learn the attitude, "Speak Lord,
thy servant heareth," command and I will obey!

In another vein, the argument has been made that when
"the high ethics of Christianity confronted the low ethics of
man," God

> tolerated some non-ideal situations and thus "condes-
> cended" to meet man on the plane of those relationships
> that were inherently honorable, and sanctify man in those
> relationships . . .[17]

The meaning intended by quoting this is that G d gave
ground to the early Christians and "winked at" the adulterous unions that existed, so that new Christians could keep
their mates with his full blessing. This tacitly admits that the
unions were illicit, else God would not have to "condescend";
but it also claims that because they were "marriages" (human-
law-only approved) they were inherently honorable! This we
deny.

A further point of the argument is that as God thus

made 'practical application' of his marriage laws to a hope-
lessly involved marriage condition, where any other course
of action would have produced a major disruption of the
social order, and would have caused a revolution by force.[18]

Our comment on this is that Jesus came not to bring
peace, but a sword. His word sets people against each other,
even family members, and truth must abide, regardless of
what the social consequences are. The word of God does
change things, and the world has historically been the better
for it. Further, it hardly behooves us to predict dire consequences, and say that God's demands are *too much* and need
to be softened. We might be like Elijah, getting all excited
about what *might* happen, without really knowing, and in
fact being wrong. We should follow the scriptures.

### Let Marriage Be In Honor

"Let marriage be held in honor among all, and let the
marriage bed be undefiled; for God will judge the immoral
and adulterous" (Hebrews 13:4). This passage is played upon
to emphasize the approvedness of *marriage,* but with definition No. 1 (see our Chapter 7) applied to the situation of
No. 2. Certainly scriptural marriage is approved, but an
adulterous union, though approved by human law and thus a
"marriage," is not what is envisioned in this passage. The last
part of the verse gives God's attitude toward adulterers, and
we need to face up to this. One author emphasizes "Marriage
is a relationship that is basically honorable,"[19] but this is not
true of a human-law marriage when the partners were not
eligible in God's sight to be married in the first place. This
type of subtle reasoning can be very dangerous for people
who are emotionally desirous of reaching a certain conclusion
anyway.

It is argued that the Hebrews 13:4 passage was addressed
to Hebrews who had known more than one ground for divorce
in their tradition, and that a rigid application of Matthew
19:9 would even void all the Jewish second-marriages (Mosaic
concession) of the early Christian converts that did not have
fornication as the grounds for their previous divorces, and

thus they all would have had to put away their mates immediately upon becoming Christians. Such a conclusion is not valid, however, for when God once recognized a particular marriage relation in one dispensation as approved, he would not change this simply because of a change in covenants. It was not a retroactive matter. If any marriage was legitimate in God's sight before the couple became Christians it would still be so afterward. What we are here discussing is *adulterous* marital unions. They were adulterous before the people were baptized, and they are still adulterous in our opinion, after baptism. Baptism, or obedience to the gospel and entrance into God's family through Christ does not change a sinful act of any kind into a blessed one any more than it obviously does not change a blessed act into a sinful one.

## The Purpose of Baptism

Baptism does several things. It brings the remission of sins; it inducts one into the Kingdom of God and into his family; it puts one into the church, etc. But there are also many things it does not do. It does not change one's race or nationality. It cleanses one from the guilt of his past sins (if he genuinely repented), but it will not change any sinful practice into a holy one. If a man is a thief, baptism will not let him keep the stolen merchandise. If he is at that time living in adultery, he will not be allowed, because of his being baptized, to continue in that activity. This ought to be clear to all.

Above all, let us emphasize once more that baptism does not exempt one from full, complete and genuine repentance, and all of the demands that such repentance makes of us.

# STUDY QUESTIONS

## Chapter 8

1. List points showing that people can "live in adultery."

2. What effort is made to try to show that the present tense of "commits adultery" does not mean "habital or repeated action"? What is the Gnomic present tense (see footnote 15)?

3. Give the gist of the Herod and David arguments, and replies.

4. What is the point about the "abiding in your calling" argument? What is wrong with it?

5. How is "marriage" wrongly defined in connection with the Hebrews 13:4 "marriage in honor" argument?

6. What about Jewish second-marriages at the time these Jews became Christians?

7. Discuss the limitation of baptism, as to what it does and does not do.

# Chapter 9

# CAN THE GUILTY PARTY REMARRY?

We now take up a new and separate problem—the status of the guilty party in a divorce granted upon the scriptural ground of fornication. It has relation to our previous problem of the person living in adultery who desires to become a Christian, in that the question of "a permanent celibacy demand" has to be determined also in this case.

Those who argue in favor of the guilty party being free to remarry[20] use a strong emotional appeal along with their reasoning. The only alternative to remarriage for these people, of course, is permanent celibacy. If God's law does not give them freedom to remarry they are "condemned" to living their entire future lives without benefit of marital blessings. Among the appeals are:

1. The demand is too rough and too severe. "From a human viewpoint, it would seem reasonable to think that every normal person could be rightfully married to someone."[21] This expression says much about the desires of the reasoner and what he is building up to.

2. The argument is made that "the innocent party would have too much power over the life of the guilty one, if a fornicator can never remarry. He could "sentence him to a celibate life for as long as he lives."[22] The argument runs on to the point that the innocent party is made to appear mean and even *guilty* if a decision for divorce should be reached. In spite of the scripture teaching, the claim is made that this is not a "rightful and lawful power."[23] It ignores the basic guilt and innocence of the parties involved.

3. The question is asked, if a fornicator cannot remarry and

53

if you should be evangelizing a stranger and learn that he is guilty of this sin, what would you do? Would you continue to try to teach him or would you say immediately that unless they gave each other up they wouldn't have a chance anyway? The answer to this is to preach the gospel to every creature and encourage them to repent of all their sins—the big ones as well as the lesser ones. God can provide answers even if we cannot see how.

4. In case we might be wrong we should be careful about making life difficult for these people. Further, they have a potential for good in the Lord's service, and we should not put a damper on that. This type of argument seems to be straining hard to make a point. It surely is more emotional than logical in justification.

5. In the past we have treated people with marital problems as second-class citizens and have given them only half-fellowship. There is no unanimity of belief on marriage doctrines. If fornication is such a sin and one that cannot be completely cleared up, we ought to learn the truth and all agree on it and "call a spade a spade" in our teaching so that people would not get involved in this. We are being unfair.

The basic biblical argument is based on the Matthew 19:9 passage—"Whosoever shall put away his wife, except for fornication, and shall marry another, committeth adultery: and he that marrieth her that is put away committeth adultery." This is reversed by these people to read "He that putteth away his wife FOR fornication, and shall marry another, doth NOT commit adultery," making it appear to be the opposite of the biblical expression above. Technically, this indicates that the phrase, "except for fornication" should also be understood to apply to the last clause of the verse and to modify "the having been put away woman." In such case it would read, "he that marrieth her that is put away EXCEPT FOR FORNICATION, committeth adultery." Though the scripture does not EXPLICITLY state it this way it is right to take it as IMPLIED, so the argument goes.

The other basic claim made in this connection is that when the innocent party is freed from the marriage bond by the fornication of his spouse, the guilty party is also freed from the same marriage bond, and since the guilty party is no longer bound by any marriage bond, he is free to be married again, just the same as the innocent party. If this were not true and the marriage tie was in some way still binding, and the innocent party married someone else, she would then be married to two persons, etc. This argument will be further elaborated in its refutation.

## Replies[2][4]

To the argument based on what might be "implied" in the last clause of Matthew 19:9, we have to say that we must go by *what is actually said*. The "implication" here is highly questionable, and too much ambiguity is raised if it be considered. What it says is that "he that marrieth her that is put away (FOR ANY REASON—JDT) committeth adultery." The scripture does NOT qualify the reason for the putting away in this clause, therefore we must not read our wishes into our thinking.

Also, the grammatical construction shows clearly that the phrase "except for fornication" is used adverbially, modifying the verb "put away" in the first clause. To claim that this phrase belongs in the final clause would call for a different construction. It could not modify the verb "marrieth" in the last clause, because no one could "marry, except for fornication," so therefore it is claimed to modify the participle, *apolelumenen* "the having been put away woman." Adverbs may sometimes modify participles but the problem here is that this participle is used as a substantive, or noun, and adverbs cannot modify nouns. Since the phrase, "except for fornication," is unquestionably an adverb in the first clause, it cannot possibly be assumed to be implied in the second clause, where it would have to be used as an adjective. The grammar ruins this argument.

As to the guilty party being made free from the marriage bond at the same time the innocent party is released from the union, the following illustration given by Deaver is apropos:

In the marriage situation there are THREE sets of hand-cuffs—not one set. The husband is handcuffed to God (to

55

the law of God); the wife is handcuffed to God (the law of God); and the husband and wife are handcuffed to each other. The marriage law is God's law, and all men are amenable to that law. When the wife is guilty of fornication the husband has the right to put away the wife—to take off the handcuffs by which he is bound to the wife. But he is still handcuffed to the law of God, and the wife (the guilty party) is still handcuffed to the law of God. The law of God allows the husband (the innocent party) to form another marriage union. But, the law of God does not allow the wife—the guilty party—to form another marriage union. The guilty party is still handcuffed to the law of God—not to the husband she sinned against.[25]

An attempt at reply to the logic of this illustration has been made:[26]

What does this bond involve? A man and a woman and God who joins them? Does it mean that they are joined to each other and to God? The Bible nowhere hints that the marriage is only for those who are loyal to God ... The truth of the matter is: a husband and wife are joined by God to each other. They are not necessarily joined to God. Marriage is a union of *a man and a woman,* not a man, a woman and God. Marriage binds a man to a woman and a woman to a man. As long as he is bound to her, she is bound to him. If he is freed from her, she is freed from him.[27]

Obviously God as a third person does not participate equally with the husband and wife in their marital relationship. But this argument must not be allowed to imply that God's LAW and his regulations do not have a definite part in a marriage union. God ordained and instituted marriage for all human beings—not just for his covenant people. And he has a say. Depending upon whether the married couple meet his laws or not, determines whether their's is an adulterous union or a blessed one. It is fallacious to argue that one would have to be "loyal" to God before his marriage laws would be binding upon them. God is strongly interested in every marriage—Christian or pagan. When a marriage is entered upon, God has a stake in it, and each party is responsible to God for how he conducts himself in the relationship.

If one spouse violates God's will by fornication and the

other is perfectly innocent, God's law on the point begins to function. At the choice of the innocent one, the union can be scripturally broken, but when this occurs it does not automatically cancel all obligations that God's law holds each person responsible for. God's law decrees that the innocent party will be without guilt in marrying someone else, but God's law has made no such provision for the guilty party. He is not released by the divorce from any of his obligations toward God.

The original marriage called for a union until death, which each spouse was obligated to uphold. The ONLY THING that can ever break the marriage bond while both parties are alive is fornication, and that ONLY FOR THE INNOCENT PARTY! "Except for fornication" is the one justifying ground for remarriage to another, but THE GUILTY PARTY DOES NOT HAVE THIS JUSTIFYING GROUND. It is possible only for the innocent spouse. The guilty one is therefore still under all obligations toward the first marriage that he ever was, in the sense of being "bound to it" by God's law. Nothing has happened to give *him* freedom! He is still "handcuffed to God's law," though not to his former wife. He still has an obligation that remains. If he should later repent, this will remove his guilt, but not his status. This is somewhat like baptism—it removes guilt but will not change other things, like one's race or nationality. Repentance on the part of a Christian fornicator can remove his guilt, but it will not allow him to continue committing the sin of adultery after his marriage ended, and he is not benefited by the "except for fornication" phrase. Therefore he would commit adultery if he remarried (Matthew 19:9).

The only reason the innocent party can remarry with God's blessing is because *God's law gives him the right,* specifically; not because "he at the moment is not tied to a marriage bond." Likewise even though the guilty party has no marriage bond, but does not have the right of remarriage from God's law, he is not free to marry again with God's approval. He is not an eligible marriage partner.

If *both* parties could remarry with God's blessing following a sin of fornication, why did Jesus discuss this at all? There is no point to it. Further, what would be the significance of the "except for fornication" phrase? It would be meaningless, if the guilty party could emerge for the divorce with the same freedom that the innocent one is granted!

Yet, again, from the teaching in Matthew 5:31, 32 we learn that the spouse who is UNJUSTLY put away is obligated to perpetual celibacy (unless the other spouse later commits adultery). So here is a clear case of God's law requiring permanent celibacy of an innocent spouse, and leaves him (or her) at the mercy of his separated companion in this respect. What justice is there, if the law of God would require perpetual celibacy in this instance of one who is totally innocent, but which would not require as much penalty of a guilty fornicator? Surely some logic ought to be seen in this.

If the guilty fornicator is free to marry again when his spouse remarries there would be nothing to prevent him "profiting from his own sin." He could deliberately plan fornication, for the purpose of getting the marriage bond broken so that he could later repent and marry again. Repentance would be next to impossible in this situation, but who is to say it would not be attempted, or has not happened? Further, a husband and wife who were unhappy with each other could plan for one of them to commit adultery for the express purpose of giving dignity to a new marriage for each of them. Knowing human beings, we would not "put it past" some to try just this sort of thing.

Probably underlying all these efforts to dignify the status of the fornicator who has violated his marriage bond—maybe even sub-consciously—lingers the feeling that permanent celibacy is just too much punishment for such a sin. As we have said earlier, sinners tend to be sympathetic with each other and are really not qualified to say how much punishment any sin deserves. We have noted that certain innocent persons clearly are required to remain celibate, and also that Jesus indicated that being a enuch for spiritual goals would for some be a highly desirable path to follow.

## STUDY QUESTIONS

### Chapter 9

1. What does it mean, that "the guilty party is free to remarry"?

2. List and discuss the several arguments made in favor of the statement being true.

3. What grammatical argument makes a difficulty for the claim?

4. Recount the "handcuff" illustration. What is its major point?

5. Discuss how one can still be bound to God's law, though free from a former spouse.

6. What is the only basis in scripture that allows divorce and remarriage? Does the guilty party have this ground?

7. Give other points of reasoning on this problem.

# Chapter 10

# DEPARTURE-I

*1 Corinthians 7:15—But if the unbelieving partner desires to separate, let it be so: in such a case the brother or sister is not bound.*

The QUESTION with which the next two chapters will come to grips is: "Does the voluntary *departure* of an alien spouse justify remarriage of the Christian?"

Some, who have concluded the answer Yes! to the above question, have called this the "Pauline Privilege," assuming that Paul allowed liberties that Jesus did not, and thus have put Paul in contradiction to Jesus, and so have created a second ground for divorce. Hopefully we shall show this term to be a mis-nomer and shall clarify the thinking adequately.

Scholarship is divided on each side of the question. We wish to be perfectly fair to both views yet do our best to seek out the truth for the plain Christian. The present chapter will present the evidence and arguments favoring the negative and reaching the answer, No! This view is held by many restoration thinkers and certainly deserves full and fair consideration. The next chapter will look at the opposing viewpoint.

### Deō-Douloō

A chief biblical argument used to support the negative conclusion is based on the word "bound" [Greek—*dedoulōtai* (lexical form, *douloō*)], the claim being that this word is not used in the New Testament to refer to "the marriage bond." The words which clearly do refer to the bondage of marriage (found in 1 Corinthians 7:27, 39 and Romans 7:2) are from the lexical form *deō*. Forms of *douloō* are used in the New Testament 128 times with several different meanings "slavery" probably being the dominant one, but "the marriage bond" is not among them, unless it is found here in v. 15. *Deō* is found 41 times, also with numerous different meanings, but three of which (those listed above) definitely refer to the bond of marriage. Since the latter fact shows that Paul uses only *deō* to reflect a clear and full reference to the marriage tie, if he had meant the matrimonial bond itself in verse 15 it seems he would have used the *deō* form instead of the *douloō* form. The different word used must, therefore, imply a different type of bondage from which the deserted Christian is freed.

In spite of a lack of unanimity on certain points, this linguistic argument, *deō* versus *douloō,* is probably the strongest argument made by those who deny that "departure" allows the Christian spouse to remarry.

## Departure

We should note here that those who answer No! to our question are almost unanimously agreed that the meaning of the word "departure" (Greek—*chorizō*) means an act of separation only from "bed and board" but it does not mean a breaking of the marriage itself. In their view this term definitely leaves room for reconciliation.

The word "departure" itself is not given much detailed study by most interpreters but it may have an important alternate meaning from the above. In one case where the word *chōrizō* is discussed [28] the meaning of v. 15 is simply equated with that of v. 11, so that reconciliation is the only option in *both* instances. A further and more precise study, therefore, seems indicated for *chōrizō.*

## Other Arguments

Verse 11 of 1 Corinthians 7 shows that where *Christian* spouses separate or cease living together, they cannot marry anyone else but must live a celibate existence (or else choose to become reconciled to each other). To compare this demand of God with the one on the Christian mate where his unbelieving spouse "departs," helps one to realize that it should not be too hard a burden on the deserted partner to live a celibate life. It should be no harder for him than for

61

the one whose spouse was a Christian. Therefore, to deny the deserted spouse the right of remarriage to a new person is considered to be not out of character with the basic teachings set forth by Paul in this context.

Following the same point, if the Christian spouse deserted by the unbeliever should be given the privilege of remarriage to a new partner, he would have a simpler and much easier obligation than the Christian who was separated from his Christian spouse, but who had to maintain a celibate existence. This difference seems unjust.

## Peace

An interesting point in our study is the meaning of "peace" in v. 15—"For God has called us to peace." What is the nature of the peace, and does this throw any light on our basic question?

One answering No!, to our question says the peace and freedom of v. 15 is the quiet and tranquility of the celibate state after the non-Christian spouse has departed. It occurs to this writer that somehow the ideal that God has called us to ought to be more than just the *absence* of family fussing and fighting. And there certainly is a void in the life of the innocent Christian who has been deserted. Celibacy is sometimes necessary but who can say it is ideal, or is true "peace"?

## Two Grounds

Another strong argument embraced by those who say, No! to our question is that if we interpret Paul to allow a valid justification for the deserted Christian's remarriage this would make *two* grounds for divorce and remarriage. Jesus gave only one, and this would then set Paul in opposition to Jesus. Further no other New Testament passage indicates that desertion is grounds for a scriptural divorce, so the safe way seems to be to opt for the one justification only— "except for fornication." This is an important matter, so we should choose what seems to be the safe course in our interpretation.

To those who conclude in the negative to our question

the above reasoning, if not overwhelming, seems certainly adequate and clear. This group includes a lot of people.

## STUDY QUESTIONS

### Chapter 10

1. What is meant by "The Pauline Privilege"?

2. Explain the central thrust of the argument on the two Greek words for "bondage," *deō* and *douloō*.

3. Give the usual interpretation of the word for departure (*chorizō*) by those who hold that the deserted Christian must remain celibate.

4. Give other arguments made in support of the same point of view.

5. Evaluate the statement that the right to remarry for the deserted Christian would make two grounds for divorce.

# Chapter 11

# DEPARTURE-II

1 Corinthians 7:15—*But if the unbelieving partner desires to separate, let it be so: in such a case the brother or sister is not bound.*

We repeat our QUESTION, which is the base topic for Chapters 10 and 11:

"Does the voluntary departure of an alien spouse justify remarriage of the Christian?"

Continuing our search, we now give the evidence and arguments favoring the affirmative and thus reaching the answer Yes!

## The Context

As we consider the contextual content of 1 Corinthians 7, and especially the earlier verses, we would like to introduce several aspects of the problem again through the words of an influential author:

(2) *Is the Christian Husband or Wife Who Has Been Maliciously Deserted by an Infidel Partner Free to Marry Again?* If not, it would be difficult to see how such "a brother or a sister is not under bondage in such cases." If they are not any longer *bound* to these deserting partners, nor *in bondage* to them, they certainly are free. If they are not free to marry again, then they are not free from this marriage bondage at all, and are, therefore, still *bound*. If Paul does not mean that the marriage bondage is broken and does not any longer exist, so far as the Christian is concerned, then his language has no meaning at all. To make it mean something else is to destroy his whole point. But someone suggests that he means that the Christian is not

64

*bound* to live with and to give the marriage privilege to such a deserting partner. That would be a wise statement from an inspired man! Even Christians could live apart, if they so desired. He has already told them to live with these heathen spouses if they can. It would now be absurd to tell them that they are under no obligation to live with those who have deserted them, and refused their companionship. How could they live with such a person? But someone else suggests that he had said in verse 10 that those who depart should remain unmarried, or be reconciled to their mate. Yes, he said that to Christians who might desire to separate. But this is to those who are deserted by heathen partners. And, since they were not able to hold these heathen mates, what would be the sense in telling Christians later to be reconciled to them? The Christian was never other than reconciled. It was the heathen that departed. Did Paul call on these heathen to remain unmarried, or to be reconciled to their Christian companions whom they, because of their religion, had deserted?

Absurd!

Then, someone is ready to say, according to that, Paul allowed divorce for desertion, whereas Christ made fornication the only ground for divorce. There is no conflict there. Desertion by a heathen includes or presupposes unfaithfulness to the partner, of course. Could anyone suppose that such a heathen, with no ideas of Christian morality, but who because of opposition to such Christian ideals deserts his partner, would live a chaste and celibate life henceforth?

Jesus said that a man who puts away his wife causes her to commit adultery. How would merely putting her away cause her to commit this sin? Would she be guilty of adultery if she lived unmarried the rest of her days? Of course not. Then how is she caused to commit adultery? *It is understood that she will find another partner,* and in doing this without being scripturally released from her husband, she is guilty of adultery. The husband caused this sin by putting her away. If, therefore, it is so well understood that a woman who is put away will marry again that Christ before mentioning a second marriage declared the woman guilty of adultery, shall we not say that Paul implied that the heathen who departs breaks the marriage bond by seeking another partner of his own kind? That is most certainly understood.

Christians might separate in order to live a pure and holy life, free from any concessions to the flesh. But Paul indicated that even they would find this too difficult, and would need to be reconciled to or come together again. Shall we assume that a heathen who forsakes his companion because of that companion's holy religion will live a holy, celibate life, or shall we know and proceed on the basis that he will form another connection? Paul assumed that he would seek another partner, and, therefore, held the Christian whom he had deserted as free from all obligation and responsibility.

With this conclusion reached, we see that Paul agrees with Christ exactly. When, therefore, he says a woman is bound to her husband as long as he lives, he must be understood to mean that this is true provided he desires to remain her husband, and does not forsake her and form a connection with another woman.

Only thus can we escape making the apostle contradict what he said in verse 15. Now, what Paul here says about a heathen would not apply to a person who is a member of some so-called "Christian denomination." Such a person, if true to his creed, believes in the Christian moralities and ideals. He might leave a member of the body of Christ, and still live a celibate life. In that case the marriage bond is not broken. Paul's language should not be interpreted as meaning that the marriage bond is broken except by unfaithfulness to the marriage vow. When a man or a woman who is worldly, who lives after the flesh, who makes no claim to Christian living, forsakes his or her companion, and stays away for years, it may be safely assumed that the bond is broken, even as Paul assumes this in reference to a heathen of his day.[29]

Following the above "opening up" of numerous angles of our question under discussion, we now wish to look at Paul's basic discussion in 1 Corinthians 7 concerning each of the three groups to whom he is giving inspired advice and instruction:

1. The single Christians, vv. 8, 9:

2. Christians married to Christians, vv. 10, 11:

3. Married couples, where one is a Christian and one is not, vv. 12-16:

Note that Paul gives *a different instruction* to each category:

8 To the unmarried and the widows I say that it is well for them to remain single as I do. 9 But if they cannot exercise self-control, they should marry. For it is better to marry than to be aflame with passion.

66

The above instruction to single Christians, is clear enough and needs no further comment here.

10 To the married I give charge, not I but the Lord, that the wife should not separate from her husband " (but if she does, let her remain single or else be reconciled to her husband) — and that the husband should not divorce his wife.

This next bit of advice (vv. 10, 11) is to Christians who are married to Christians and the Lord's will for them is, "no divorce at all." If they perchance need to live separately they are still married to each other and their only option is reconciliation or continued celibacy. They cannot marry anyone else. In verse 11 note the two verbs—"separate" (Greek—*chōrizō*) and "divorce" (Greek—*aphienai*) which apparently have the same meaning, as one is applied to one spouse and the other to the second spouse, with the same significance.

12 To the rest I say, not the Lord, that if any brother has a wife who is an unbeliever, and she consents to live with him, he should not divorce her. " If any woman has a husband who is an unbeliever, and he consents to live with her, she should not divorce him. " For the unbelieving husband is consecrated through his wife, and the unbelieving wife is consecrated through her husband. Otherwise, your children would be unclean, but as it is they are holy. " But if the unbelieving partner desires to separate, let it be so; in such a case the brother or sister is not bound.

In verses 12-15, "to the rest" means instruction for everybody else under the influence of Paul's instruction to Christians, which is obviously then limited to such Christians as were married to non-Christians. The scriptural advice to this group is *not the same* as to those wedded couples of vv. 10, 11, where both are Christians, but is necessarily *different* instruction, otherwise there would be no point in having this third group—he would have included them as recipients of the instruction of verses 10 and 11.

However, those answering No! to our question reach the conclusion that Christians who are deserted by unbelieving spouses have the *same* demand laid on them by God's will as ' the Christian husbands and wives of verse 11. If separated, they must remain unmarried.

This point, that since Paul speaks to three separate categories and obviously gives separate instructions to each (otherwise it is pointless to divide them into three groups instead of two) has apparently escaped the notice of many students of this passage. It is the key, however, that should make us see that we should seek the *different* advice given to those Christians who have non-Christian spouses. This *different* instruction is that if their non-Christian spouse voluntarily *departs*, "they are not under bondage in such cases."

The above observations are no doubt why Brewer and others conclude that "in such cases," the *departure* is of such a nature that the deserted Christian *may legitimately assume adultery*, without having to wait for absolute proof, such as a private detective, for example, might be expected to bring in, and therefore the Christian, in such cases, is free to remarry. They are, this conclusion holds, free from the marriage bond, and if so are certainly free to remarry.

Implications and further aspects of the above reasoning will be discussed later. Next, however, we turn to the linguistic aspects of the words *bondage (douloō)*, and *depart (chōrizō)* for a somewhat thorough analysis. After all, the exegesis of the Greek text is what we finally have to go by. All interpretive reasoning and theories about any passage have to square with what the Bible itself says, and that is determined by sound exegesis.

As we indicated earlier the use of the two words for "bondage" *(deō* and *douloō)* is the fulcrum of the best argument in our judgment made for the answer No! to our question. A strong effort is made to keep the meaning of these words separate and distinct, with *deō* used for the bond of matrimony, while *douloō* (most frequent meaning, the bondage of slavery) for some other kind of bondage.[30] The reasoning says that Paul could not have meant the matrimonial bond in v. 15 since he used *douloō* (grammatical form —*dedoulōtai*). In this case, therefore, the deserted Christian spouse "is not under some kind of bondage or other"; but IS STILL UNDER THE MARRIAGE BOND, so that remarriage to someone else is not possible. This interpretation, then, would make the obligation on the Christian spouse deserted by the unbeliever to be EXACTLY THE SAME obligation as that of the Christian spouses of v. 11 who, if separated, must live celibately. In such a case, therefore, there would be no point in having any third category or group to receive marital instruction in this context. Further, the statement, "in such a case the brother or sister is not bound" would make no sense whatever, if they too must remain celibate like the Christians of v. 11. If no third category is to be understood and the case of verses 13-15 is to be considered as the same as that of verses 10, 11, then we obviously could add the statement "the brother or sister who has been departed from is not under bondage in such cases" to the material in verses 10 and 11. But no one would want to do this, since verses 10 and 11 expressly say that they "must remain unmarried"—the exact opposite of "not being under bondage."

We would observe, however, that the words *deō* and *douloō* may not be as different from each other as has been made out. They both refer to a *bondage,* and each word has several different meanings, as most words do. In the New Testament *deō* is the word most commonly used to speak of the matrimonial tie (or binding), and *douloō* generally is used to refer to slavery—both literal and figurative. It would be wrong, however, to say that they never could mean the same, and could therefore never be used in the same context as synonyms. Paul does this with other words.

An illustration of the varied uses of words, note that the word "married" is used by Paul to mean both approved and disapproved unions (cf. our Chapters 1, 3 and 7 above); the word "holy" in v. 14 here, as applied to the children of the mixed marriage, does not mean its usual sense of "Christian." *Douloō* does not always mean *slavery,* as in 1 Corinthians 9:19, "I brought myself under bondage (Greek form—*edoulōsa*) to all that I might gain the more," it means an obligation or tie that differs from slavery. Likewise Titus 2:3, "Bid the older women likewise to be reverent in behavior, not to be slanderers or slaves *(dedoulomenas)* to drink" indicates an obligation different from literal slavery.

*Deō* likewise has other meanings than the bond of marriage, as in Revelation 20:2 *"bound* him a thousand years"; Acts 21:33, *"bound* with two chains," *et cetera.*

R. C. Trench's *Synonyms of the Greek New Testament* is an entire book of words that have the same meanings in certain contexts as other words. This phenomenon is so common that it need not be belabored.

Synonyms used with the same (identical) meaning in our context are *(chōrizō)* "separate" (v. 10) and "divorce" *(aphienai)* in verse 11, and the same words subsequently through verse 15. Also, "asunder" *(chōrizō)* of Matthew 19:6 and "divorce" *(apoluō)* of Matthew 19:9 are exact synonyms in that context.

In the light of the above and *for purposes of our study* we are here going to consider that the *dedoulōtai* of verse 15 refers to *the marriage bond itself,* bound to each other and bound to God's law also—both sets of handcuffs, and that therefore this is what the deserted Christian is freed from. This concept will be elaborated later.

To show that there is not "all that much difference" between *deō* and *douloō,* note that Liddell and Scott's lexicon of Classical Greek (8th edition) shows that "perhaps" the *douloō* forms (here the noun *doulos*) are originally derived from the root for *deō* —

δοῦλος, ὁ : (perh. from δέω *to bind,* cf. *bond-man,* Pers. *bendeh* ):— properly, *a born bondman* or *slave,* opp. to *one made a slave* (ἀνδράποδον), Thuc. 8. 28 ; then, generally, *a bondman, slave,* opp. to δεσπότης, Hdt., etc.: Hom. has only the fem. δούλη, ἡ, *a bondwoman* (cf. δώλα):— often also of the Persians and other nations subject to a despot, Hdt., etc. ; οὔ τινος δοῦλοι κέκληνται, of the Greeks, Aesch. Pers. 242 ; cf. δουλεία, δουλόω:—χρημάτων δ. *slavery to money,* Eur. Hec. 865 ; so, γνάθου δ. Id. Fr. 284. 5 ; λιχνειῶν, λαγνειῶν Xen. Oec. 1, 22, cf. Mem. I. 3, 11 : cf. οἰκέτης.     II. as Adj., δοῦλος, η, ον, like Lat. *servus, slavish, servile, subject,* δούλη πόλις Soph. O. C. 917, Xen. Mem. 4. 2, 29 ; γνώμαισι δούλαις Soph. Tr. 53 ; δ. ἔχειν βίον Ib. 302 ; σῶμα δ. Id. Fr. 677; τοὺς τρόπους δούλους παρασχεῖν Eur. Supp. 876 ; δ. θάνατος, ζυγόν, πούς Id. ; (never so in Aesch.) ; δ. καὶ τυραννουμένη πόλις Plat. Rep. 577 D ; δ. ἡδοναί = δουλοπρεπεῖς, Ib. 587 C etc.;—Comp. δου-λότερος *more of a slave,* Hdt. 7. 7.     2. τὸ δοῦλον = οἱ δοῦλοι, Eur. Ion 983, etc.; also *slavery, a slavish life,* Ib. 556.     3. *subordinate,* δ. ἐπιστῆμαι Arist. Metaph. 2. 2, 7.

Also Thayer's lexicon says that *most* scholars accept that *douloō* is derived from the root, *deō*.

δοῦλος, -η, -ον, (derived by most fr. δέω to tie, bind; by some fr. ΔΕΛΩ to ensnare, capture, [(?) al. al.; cf. Vaniček p. 322]); *serving, subject to:* παρεστήσατε τὰ μέλη ὑμῶν δοῦλα τῇ ἀκαθαρσίᾳ, Ro. vi. 19. Then substantively, ἡ δούλη *a female slave, bondmaid, handmaid:* τοῦ θεοῦ, τοῦ κυρίου, one who worships God and submits to him, Acts ii. 18 (fr. Joel ii. 29 (iii. 2)); Lk. i. 38, 48. ὁ δοῦλος, Sept. for עֶבֶד; 1. *a slave, bondman, man of*

Thus if *deō* and *douloō* are close enough in meaning to have come from the same root word originally, their use in overlapping service as synonyms in a single context is not at all surprising or strange. This would indicate that the strong concern to keep them separate in meaning in every context is unjustified.

We next note some lexical references which show a "general bondage" meaning for *douloō,* as in Thayer:

δουλόω, -ῶ : fut δουλώσω; 1 aor. ἐδούλωσα; pf. pass. δεδούλωμαι; 1 aor. pass. ἐδουλώθην; (δοῦλος); [fr. Aeschyl. and Hdt. down]; *to make a slave of, reduce to bondage;* a. prop.: τινά, Acts vii. 6; τούτῳ καὶ [yet T WH om. Tr br. καὶ] δεδούλωται to him he has also been made a bondman, 2 Pet. ii. 19. b. metaph.: ἐμαυτόν τινι give myself wholly to one's needs and service, make myself a bondman to him, 1 Co. ix. 19 ; δουλοῦσθαί τινι, to be made subject to the rule of some one, e. g. τῇ δικαιοσύνῃ, τῷ θεῷ, Ro. vi. 18, 22 ; likewise ὑπό τι, Gal. iv. 3 ; δεδουλωμένος οἴνῳ, wholly given up to, enslaved to, Tit. ii. 3 (δουλεύειν οἴνῳ, Liban. epist. 319) ; δεδούλωμαι ἔν τινι, to be under bondage, held by constraint of law or necessity, in some matter, 1 Co. vii. 15. [COMP.: κατα-δουλόω.] *

Greenfield's Lexicon, in one edition of which this writer once noted that *deō* and *douloō* are from the same root (but which edition is not presently available), shows similar meanings for these two Greek words. (note the underlining):

Δέω, f. δήσω, p. δέδεκα, a. 1. ἔδησα, p. pass. δέδεμαι, a. 1. pass. ἐδέθην, to bind, tie, Mat. 13. 30; 21. 2, et al.; to bin.1, confine, Mat. 27. 2; 14. 3, et al.; to impede, hinder, 2 Ti. 2. 9; to affe~t with disease, Lu. 13. 16; to bind *by a legal or moral tie, as mar-riage,* Ro. 7. 2. *Jo. 7. 27, 39; by impt.* to impel, compel, Ac. 20. 22; *in N. T.,* to pronounce or declare any thing to be binding or obliga-tory; *or,* to declare any thing pro-hibited and unlawful, Mat. 16. 19; 18. 18.

Δουλόω, ῶ, f. ώσω, a. 1. ἐδούλωσα, p. pass. δεδούλωμαι, a. 1. pass. ἐδου-λώθην, to reduce to servitude, enslave, oppress by retaining in servitude, Ac. 7. 6. 2 Pe. 2. 19; *met.* to render subservient, 1 Co. 9. 19; *pass.* to be under restraint, 1 Co. 7. 15; to be in bondage, *spiritually or morally,* Gal. 4. 3. Tit. 2. 3; to become devoted to the service of, Ro. 6. 18, 27.

Also Kittel's *Theological Dictionary of the New Testament,* the most comprehensive of today's lexicons, shows that the meaning of *douloō* in the New Testament is "always figurative" and that in 1 Corinthians 7:15 it means a "total binding," which would therefore include the entire matri-monial bond.

δουλόω, καταδουλόω.

Both terms are common from the time of Herodotus and the tragic dramatists and are found in the LXX, where καταδουλόω is to some extent a stronger form of δουλόω. The basic meaning is "to make a slave," "to enslave." The words are used either literally to denote absolute subjection or the loss of autonomy (Hdt., I, 94 and 174; Thuc., I, 98; 1 Macc. 8:10; Epict. Diss., I, 19, 9; ⇒ a.), or figuratively (τὰς ψυχάς, Isocr., 12, 78; ἡ τύχη τὸ σῶμα κατεδουλώσατο, Philemo, 95, 8 [CAF, II, 508; 4/3 cent. B.C.]; ⇒ b.).

Except in Ac. 7:6, where Gn. 15:13 LXX is quoted and δουλοῦν refers to the enslavement of Israel by the Egyptians (→ 266), the NT always uses the terms in sense b. and therefore figuratively. Two groups may be distinguished, the one in which the words are used in a secular context and the other in which they form part of the religious use of the word group.

In 1 C. 7:15 δουλοῦν expresses total binding by another. When in a mixed marriage the unbelieving partner seeks divorce, οὐ δεδούλευται ὁ ἀδελφὸς ἢ ἡ ἀδελφὴ ἐν τοῖς τοιούτοις. [1] In relation to Jn. 8:34 (→ 274) we have a kind of definition of δοῦλος in 2 Pt. 2:19: ᾧ γάρ τις ἥττηται, τούτῳ δεδούλωται. Paul adopts a similar use of δοῦλος (→ 277) in 1 C. 9:19 when he says of himself with

Next, we note Vincent's *Word Studies* on 1 Corinthians 7:15:

15. Is not under bondage (οὐ δεδούλωται). A strong word, indicating that Christianity has not made marriage a state of slavery to believers. Compare δέδεται *is bound,* ver. 39, a milder word. The meaning clearly is that wilful desertion on the part of the unbelieving husband or wife sets the other party free. Such cases are not comprehended in Christ's words.

and Lenski's Commentary:

Paul writes succinctly: χωριζέσθω, "let him keep himself separate!" Short and done with. What can, indeed, be done when an unbeliever takes such action? The marriage is ended; let it remain thus. While Paul writes ὁ ἀνὴρ ὁ ἄπιστος, we see that he has in mind both cases, an unbelieving husband deserting his believing wife, an unbelieving wife deserting her believing husband. What is now the status of such a believing spouse? "The brother or the sister has not been placed in bondage ἐν τοῖς τοιούτοις, in such circumstances." The verb is placed emphatically forward and is itself strong: "not has been enslaved the brother or the sister."

The perfect tense states more than the present used in our versions. The perfect reaches back to the day when the unbelieving spouse entered upon the desertion and states that from that moment onward the believing spouse has not been held bound. From that day onward the fetters of the marriage tie have been broken and remain so, now and indefinitely. The deserting spouse broke them. No law binds the believing spouse. Let us add that no odium on the part of Christians has a right to bind such a believing, deserted spouse. It goes without saying that a believing spouse will by Christian kindness and persuasion do all that can be done to prevent a rupture. But when these fail, Paul's verdict is: "Thou art free!"

Desertion is exactly like adultery in its effect. Both disrupt the marriage tie. For that matter, the case is the same as when in olden times a wife was forced out of the home by her husband. The essence of marriage is union. When this is disrupted the union which God

The sum total of information from these lexicons, word studies, and the commentary is very formidable in favor of the "bondage" of 1 Corinthians 7:15 being in fact the total marriage bond. If the deserted Christian is "not under bondage" "in such cases," then of course he is free to remarry. If he is not free to remarry, then he is still "under bondage."

There are many, however, who hold that the bondage is

of another kind, with several options being offered, as noted in Note No. 30. We recognize the claims of this position, but feel that the evidence given above carries much weight and must be answered if our conclusion is really wrong.

## Chōrizō

Another lexical word about which there is a difference of opinion is that of "departure" or "separation" (Greek—Chōrizō)—whether it means mere leaving (or the quitting of bed and board), or an absolute and complete divorce and dissolving of the marital bond.

We have already observed that in verse 11 "separation" *(chōrizō)* and "divorce" *(aphienai)* are used synonomously—one to one spouse and the other to the other spouse. In this case it would appear that the separation was therefore total.

R. L. Roberts, Jr. has done a scholarly investigation[31] of our problem and in our judgment he forcefully shows that *chōrizō* in this context clearly means a breaking of the total marriage bond itself:

*Chōrizō* is used four times in this context with reference to the marriage relationship. It is also used by the Lord in the statement "What God hath joined together, let not man *put asunder*" (Matt. 19:6; Mark 10:9).[1] This word is formed by the use of the adverbial preposition *chōris* ("separate, apart, or by itself"), which became the tense-stem to which is added the suffix -*izo*.[2] The word resulting is intensive or iterative; that is, it expresses the idea of separation more intensively than does the adverb.

Originally the word seems to have been used as a reference to mere separation or division of any sort, but by the fourth century B. C. it had come to be used also of marital separation or divorce. The Greek orator Isaeus (8,36) (420-350 B. C.) and Polybius (31:26) (second century B. C.) used the word in the sense of divorce.[3] Arndt and Gingrich state that *chōrizō* is found often "in marriage contracts in the papyri" and cite one reference of this use in a second century B. C. papyrus *(PSI* 166, 11) and three references to first century B. C. papyri *(BGU* 1101, 5; 1102, 8; 1103, 6) where the same use occurs. Based on these uses their claim is that the passive (or middle) form means "a. *separate* (oneself), *be separated* of divorce" and conclude that Paul's use of the same word in I Corinthians 7:11-15 is that of absolute separation in divorce.

Moulton and Milligan say that "the word has almost become a technical term in connexion with divorce, as in Corinthians 7:10, 11,

74

15."[4] They cite several illustrations including: *can de diaphoras autois genamenēs chōrizontai ap' allēlō* . . ., "but if any difference arises between them and they separate the one from the other . . ." *(BGU* I. 251[6], A. D. 81).

Adolf Deissmann says of *chōrizomai* that it is used in the Fayyum Papyri as in I Corinthians 7:10, 11, 15 and is a "technical expression for divorce." He further says that "in marriage-contracts there are usually conditions for the possibility of separation; these are introduced by the formula *can de (hoi gamountes) chōrizōntai ap' allēlōn"*—"But if (the married) separate from one another . . ."[5]

It would seem certain from this evidence and the context of I Cor. 7:10ff that the word as used by Paul here refers to the separation of divorce. It is not just separation in "bed and board" but of the legal dissolution of the marriage bond.[6]

---

[1]The word is used in a non-marriage situation simply of separation in distance in Acts 1:4; 18:1, 2; Rom. 8:35, 89; Phile. 15; and Heb. 7:26 ("separated from sin").

[2]A. T. Robertson and W. H. Davis, *A New Short Grammar of the Greek New Testament* (New York: Harper & Brothers, 1936), pp. 113, 179.

[3]W. F. Arndt and F. W. Gingrich, *Greek-English Lexicon of the New Testament and Other Early Christian Literature* (Chicago: University of Chicago Press, 1957). Art. *Chōrizō.*

[4]James Moulton and George Milligan, *The Vocabulary of the Greek Testament* (Grand Rapids: Wm. B. Eerdman's Pub. Co., 1959).

[5]Adolph Deissmann, *Bible Studies* (Edinburgh, T. & T. Clark, 1923), p. 247. Diessmann cites *BU* 251[6] as above, together with 252[7] (98 A. D.), PER. XXIV. 27 (136 A. D.), XXVII. 16 (190 A. D.).

[6]Many other instances could be produced. Liddell-Scott, *Greek English Lexicon* (9th Ed., 1940) cite Polybius (31. 23. 11) in the passive *kechōrismenē apo tou andros, "divorced,"* and a fragment from Euripides (1063.13) of a wife *thasson . . . oistou . . . chōrizetai.*

Note Robert's observing that Liddell and Scott indicate that *chōrizō* means "divorce" as a more or less technical, common term when used in the passive.

Now, if *chōrizō* in our context does mean a real, complete divorce, originated and carried out by the unbeliever, and if the brother or sister is "in such cases not under bondage," it would seem that they are totally freed from that marriage and can scripturally enter another (except to whatever degree any other passages of scripture might have a bearing).

## Other Observations

To say, however, that mere desertion alone serves as adequate and scriptural grounds for divorce to the Christian is really not the story. In such a case adultery on the part of the unbeliever is assumed, so that there are *NOT two grounds for divorce,* and Jesus and Paul then teach the same thing. No doubt if the deserted Christian spouse should hire a private detective to follow the departed unbeliever around it would not be long before evidence of adultery would be available, since the unbeliever has no regard for God's marriage law and is a normal human being.

All this interpretation is doing, therefore, is to say that Paul's instruction merely saves the deserted Christian the time and trouble of obtaining absolute evidence of adultery.

Is it unwise or unscriptural to *assume* adultery on the part of the departed unbeliever? No, for Jesus *assumed* it on the part of the Christian spouse unjustly put away when he said, "everyone who divorces his wife, except on the ground of unchastity, makes her an adulteress (Matthew 5:32). When put away she is innocent, and in no way could she be an adulteress until she commits the act. So Jesus' words have to *assume* that she will do just that. Jesus did not say, "if she remarries," but he said, "makes her an adulteress," which statement could not be true except for the assumption that she would remarry or enter some other sexual union. Also, Paul's instruction to married Christians (1 Corinthians 7:4, 5), indicates the difficulty of living celibate for a long time, for normal people who do not have a special gift of continency.

Further, when one *scripturally* divorces a spouse for adultery, how much evidence must we have and how specific must his evidence be? Must he have photographic evidence? Surely not, so even where one puts a spouse away scripturally it involves some circumstantial evidence, which is the same thing as making some assumptions. If Paul, then in v. 15 assumes the departed unbeliever will go out and commit adultery, this is no strange matter.

Even Christian spouses can live apart (vv. 10, 11). If then, this is all that is open to the deserted Christian, we would not need the instruction "to the rest" of vv. 12-15. In the case of the mixed marriage the Christian was never anything but reconciled, so we conclude that the instruction to the Christian spouse in a mixed marriage (vv. 12-15) is a *different message* than that where both partners are Christians (vv. 10, 11).

A further important idea may be found in the word "unbeliever." If the spouse who "departed" was a Bible-believing member of some present day denomination who respected God's marriage law and if his "departure" was simply moving to a boarding house across the street where he could be observed daily, and if there were never the slightest reason to suspect adultery, the present writer holds that he has not absolutely "departed," and that the Christian spouse would therefore have no grounds for remarriage—since adultery could not truly be assumed. *There is,* in fact, *only one scriptural ground for divorce and remarriage—fornication!* The evidence may be absolute, or in some cases based on a legitimate assumption, but fornication must be there as the basic ground to justify a Christian's remarriage.[32]

# STUDY QUESTIONS

## Chapter 11

1. What impact does the long quotation at the beginning of the chapter make on your thinking? List some points.

2. List and discuss Paul's advice or instruction to each of the three groups in 1 Corinthians 7:8-15. Comment on the differences between them.

3. What advice do those answering No! to the basic question understand Paul to be giving to groups two and three of this passage?

4. How important is it that the instruction be different to each of the three groups?

5. Discuss the question of the innocent party assuming adultery. What passages throw further light on the idea?

6. Give the discussion of the *deō–douloō* relationship as presented in this chapter. What would this mean, if true?

7. How common are synonyms in the New Testament?

8. Comment on the lexical support for *deō* and *douloō* being synonyms in Chapter 7?

9. What evidence is there for *chōrizō* meaning a separation of the marriage bond?

10. What if there is good reason to believe that the departed unbeliever will not commit adultery?

# Chapter 12

# SUMMARY AND CONCLUSIONS

God has given us adequate information on sex, marriage, and morals but there is yet much ignorance of his will. Man's physical temptations are great and the increasing worldliness and lack of spiritual concern in the present age has stepped up the tempo of sin and even Christians are drawn into Satan's web in large numbers.

There is so much emotion that surrounds marriage, sex and the birth of children that most people who get caught in the web of this type of sin to any degree are no longer able to use rational thought and tend to make all decisions on the basis of blind emotion. Friends, relatives, preachers, elders, and all of us are drawn into this emotional matrix and tend to have strong personal desires concerning the conclusions we want to obtain as to what God's will is. There could be a strong suspicion that some of us *want* a certain situation so much that we even look for "loopholes" in the biblical teaching. Let us hope that this is not really true of any of us. We should realize that the things of the spirit must control our basic lives rather than our carnal desires.

God's original law was that marriage is for life—one man for one woman. Moses was permitted to make a temporary concession but Jesus restored the original pattern, with the single exceptive proviso that adultery would be valid grounds for divorce and remarriage, FOR THE INNOCENT PARTY, in case he or she could not see fit to forgive the guilty, but now penitent, spouse. The "marriage till death" demand seems reasonable when we understand that the twain actually becomes one flesh. This is not just a legalistic mechanical process, but hopefully, when saturated by love and trust, will produce two lives of outstanding beauty and joy as they tread down the pathway of life as one flesh in reality.

Paul's teaching, especially prominent in 1 Corinthians 7, gives more detail in numerous points and thus complements, but does not contradict, the teaching of Jesus. There are practical applications, but marriage is still until death, and there is only one divinely approved ground upon which divorce can be approved—fornication, where "the twain" is invaded.

Human law may or may not coincide with God's law. God's law is what determines sin—not what happens at the courthouse. All people everywhere are obligated to God's laws, including his laws of marriage. Some are in special covenant relationships with God from time to time but the non-covenant people also are capable of sin and become guilty of sin. It should be obvious that aliens can and do commit fornication as well as many other types of sin. Sodom and Gomorrah and Nineveh illustrate the non-covenant sinners.

Repentance is a must before any sin can be forgiven. It is a change of will which is big enough to bring about a change of conduct. The change of conduct involves restitution of the original status insofar as it is possible. In no way can the penitent sinner keep the fruit of his sin.

In determining God's will we must recognize that it comes only through the Bible and that its statements must be interpreted by rational and scholarly techniques rather than by subjective intuitions and emotional bias.

Early church history is valuable for confirmatory information on interpretation but cannot, of itself establish divine authority on any point. The authority can reside only in the New Testament. Oftentimes in marginal matters church history can give clarification, but its services are limited to clarification and confirmation.

It is not valid interpretation to cite "emotionally charged consequences" as reasons why God's will cannot be thus and so. Truth must prevail, regardless of where "the chips may fall." We must not imagine that such and such cannot be God's will since it would have a negative effect on innocent children. This is "emotion over logic." God's law, man's law and natural law all punish their violators regardless of who may suffer as a part of the consequences.

A claim that is played upon heavily in this connection is that when an alien is baptized into Christ his baptism not only "washes away" his past sins but it somehow sanctifies his existing marriage so that if it has been an adulterous union it now becomes a blessed one. This strange doctrine overrates what baptism was ever purposed to do. Nothing in God's word that this writer knows of can turn a sinful act into a holy one—especially without full and complete repentance.

It is shown in Chapter 8 that persons can "live in adultery." Herod was condemned for it by John the Baptist. David's marriage to Bathsheba was after her husband was dead, so their marriage was not living in adultery.

The argument about abiding in the calling of 1 Corinthians 7:20 obviously does not apply to sinful callings, but rather to temporal and civil relationships of life. It would not expect one to abide in homosexuality, for example, nor in idolatry or covetousness. Neither can one involved in adultery use this passage as divine authority for "abiding in" this particular sin.

The appeal to Hebrews 13:4—"Let marriage be held in honor among all"—is made as though any and all marriages are considered by God as honorable. But we learned in Chapter 7 that the Bible uses the word "married" to apply to divinely approved ones and also to certain adulterous unions. The hope here is to get adulterous marriages of aliens counted as "honorable" but this is not possible. The passage applies only to non-sinful marriages, and the rest of the verse, "let the marriage bed be undefiled; for God will judge the immoral and adulterous," indicates the situation into which adulterous unions fit.

The question, raised by some, about whether the guilty party of a "divorce for fornication," is not also freed to remarry at the same time the innocent party is freed to do this, ignores the fact of both parties being obligated to God's law. The innocent party is freed when fornication occurs according to Matthew 19:9, but there is no passage anywhere that grants such freedom to the guilty party. So, when the parties are freed from each other, the guilty one is still obligated to God's law. He is not in a position to benefit from the "except for fornication" phrase, and is therefore obligated to celibacy.

In the entirely different problem concerning the status of the Christian who is deserted by his unbelieving spouse (1 Corinthians 7:12-15), there are many who hold that the Christian is obligated to permanent celibacy. Chief among the arguments used are the distinction between two Greek words for bondage—*deō* and *douloō,* the first one used of the marriage bond and the second one most commonly used of slavery, either literal or figurative. *Douloō* is used in v. 15, where one might expect *deō* if the marriage tie is the "bondage" under consideration.

A further consideration is that Paul would be arrayed against Jesus and there would be two grounds for divorce and remarriage if the deserted Christian is free to remarry.

Arguments for the deserted Christian being "not under (marriage) bondage" and thus free to remarry include:

1. Paul's instruction to this category is obviously *different* from that to the married Christians of vv. 10, 11, but the latter can opt only for reconciliation or celibacy. If the above view is true the instruction would be the same for both groups.

2. Adultery is here assumed on the part of the separating unbeliever. This is not far-fetched as Jesus assumed it of the innocent wife put away unjustly (Matthew 5:32).
   Of course time is required before such adultery will occur, and if there is good reason to believe it will not occur then there is no valid departure and the Christian would not be free to remarry. Desertion alone is not grounds for divorce and remarriage. There must be a good basis for assuming adultery.

3. *Deō* and *douloō* are apparently from the same basic root word and therefore as cognates may well be synonyms on occasion, as many words are. Their sharp separateness needed by the opposing argument seems unjustified. Even the word *chōrizō,* separate, or depart, is often

82

used for complete divorce and the breaking of the marriage bond itself. Jesus used the word in Matthew 19:6–"What God hath joined together, let no man put asunder." The putting asunder *(chorizeto)* is actually the opposite of the "joining together" and so clearly means a breaking of the marriage bond itself.

Thus it would seem that on two counts, *chorizo* and *douloo,* we are speaking in v. 15 of a total separation, and in which case the deserted Christian is no longer "under bondage" and thus is free to remarry, "in such cases."

Our conclusions, in the light of the entire study, may be briefly stated:

1. Marriage is beautiful and is the best life except for those Christians with a special gift of continence. It is for life—the twain become one flesh.

2. Fornication (adultery) is the one and only ground for divorce and remarriage. Those without this ground must work at reconciliation where possible, otherwise celibacy is the only option.

3. The alien is responsible to God's marriage law and can commit adultery. He must repent of this and stop the relationship if he becomes a Christian.

4. Early church history in and of itself does not convey divine authority. It is valuable for clarification and confirmation in many ways.

5. Consequences, however emotional or tender, do not negate sin and its punishment.

6. Baptism does not sanctify an adulterous marriage. If it is adulterous before baptism, the same union will be adulterous afterward.

7. The guilty party in a divorce for fornication has only the option of celibacy.

8. The Christian whose unbelieving spouse fully "departs" may assume adultery in a reasonable time (unless there are good reasons why adultery should not be assumed) and in such a case is not under bondage and therefore is

free to remarry. [This really means he has no obligation to hire a detective to bring in hard evidence of adultery. If the departed unbeliever is a worldly person and may reasonably be expected to act as normal worldly people do, the Christian may in a reasonable time assume adultery, and in such a case he is totally free from the marriage bond.]

## STUDY QUESTIONS

### Chapter 12

1. Discuss the current moral malaise.

2. What is dangerous about extremely heavy emotional involvements and being a Christian?

3. Review God's law of marriage—
   • at the first
   • during Moses' law
   • as given by Jesus
   • as outlined by Paul

4. Briefly show that an alien can commit adultery.

5. What are the demands of repentance?

6. Of what value is a knowledge of early church history?

7. Discuss the idea that baptism sanctifies an adulterous marriage.

8. Comment on "abiding in one's calling," and "Let marriage be held in honor."

9. Give the major reason why the guilty party is not free to remarry.

10. Review the arguments, pro and con, for the deserted Christian spouse being free to remarry. What does the idea of assuming adultery have to do with this?

# Chapter 13

# RESPONSIBILITIES OF LEADERS

In view of the sexual revolution and the crumbling morality of the present age it devolves upon the elders and other leaders of the local churches to face up to the problems and to resolve to stem the tide as best they can for the sake of the souls involved and for the cause of Christ.

Probably every congregation has the sin of adultery being practiced openly, with no one doing anything about it. The reason may be ignorance—on the part of the participants or perchance of the leadership.

Maybe the leaders are simply confused, and although they know that what is going on is wrong they do not know how to attack it. Perchance they are not sure enough about God's will to know just what to do. Maybe they have been accustomed to this situation for so long that they are worn down and have given up any hope of bucking the tide.

Some leaders have members of their own families who are guilty of this sin, or perchance prominent persons who are their close friends. Maybe they have been "turned off" by other leaders who wanted to deal with the problem with heavy authoritarianism.

All of us can understand and sympathize with the hardships that people may be called upon to endure as they take steps to get their lives straight, but we should not let this cause us to fail to stand firmly for truth and right.

Above all we must not take the line of least resistance or look for easy solutions. Too many of us have dreaded to face reality as God's leaders, and so, in fact, have done nothing.

Preachers have hesitated to preach on divorce and remarriage because they know of opposition that would spring up.

We have been dilatory too long!

"Rise up, O Men of God!"

### Teaching

A first step in handling the problem is to plan a thorough teaching program so that all, from young and old, will know God's will.

The young people should have it drilled into them from an early age that marriage is "until death." They should be warned about ill-advised marriages in general and problems that can arise, but especially about the dangers of marrying a divorcee.

Adults need the teaching because little has been done on the subject through the years.

The teaching should be done in classes, in sermons, through counseling sessions and an excellent way that is new to us is the Marriage Enrichment Seminar, done for large groups by specialists.

The content of the instruction should include all of the biblical teaching about marriage and divorce and remarriage, but also all the advice and counseling that has been developed to help good Christians make their marriages to approach the ideal. This latter thrust will do much to eliminate divorces, and this would stop our problem at its beginning.

Teaching on this topic should be more or less constant, for new young people as they grow into the age of understanding, and as new adults who do not know the truth enter the congregation. Visitors to services might be helped greatly.

People who are caught in the divorce problem should be taught and dealt with in a tender and loving way. The fact of our love for them should be obvious. Their lives are shattered.

They must have sympathy and understanding if we are to be able to help them.

We should teach, teach, teach until we are sure the people know.

## Counseling Attitudes

Not everyone should try to counsel or work out problems as delicate as divorce and remarriage can be. The attitude of the counselor or elder is all important. The following are crucial:

1. One should hate sin but he must love the sinner. This is not always easy to do.

2. Kindness, patience, tenderness and loving concern must always be prominent, yet should not replace a firm concern for the truth and right.

3. The attitude should ever be prayerful. It is a big burden to be involved in regulating the lives of other people. One seemingly small error might do great harm. No human can act in the place of God.

4. One should be courageous and not cowards toward the problem, but in a wholesome self-effacing way.

5. Above all, he should avoid a spirit of authoritarianism. There is no place for "bossiness."

## Handling the Problems

Church leaders should learn the teaching of the book before they try to convey it to others. You cannot teach what you do not know.

A fallacy that has afflicted a few newly appointed elders is that upon their appointment they have assumed that they were infallibly knowledgeable on every point. They do not necessarily feel that the Holy Spirit imparts information to them as needed but possibly that they had it when appointed. At least the assumption is that as elders they do not need to study or do research—and this is the big fallacy.

When appointed, it is generally assumed that elders have the capacity for good judgment. But learning the truth and collecting the facts still have to be done. Men are not automatically "guided into all truth" today, and probably the biggest bane of elders today is that they do not continually study—to learn better how to do their work. They should be students of the word. They should study all kinds of religious literature. They should read appropriate religious journals to know what is going on and what current problem areas are.

As to collecting the facts, experience aids here but research techniques and methods will be invaluable when applied rightly. Thoroughness is urgent. Do not settle for a few facts but keep digging until you get all you can. Many points may not seem relevant but later on one of them could be the major fact that proves the case.

In trying to learn, for example, whether a spouse actually committed adultery when all you have is circumstantial evidence, it may be impossible to know *for sure*. In such case elders must not do the deciding—it must be left up to the "innocent" spouse because it is his soul being risked if the decision is wrong. Elders must recognize their limitations.

Once the total truth is determined as to what the real condition of the involved individuals are, then one is in position to teach and inform them of these facts. In case they sinned in ignorance or in the face of wrong teaching they should be counseled with much love and tenderness. There is never any point in hurting people unnecessarily and driving them into a worse condition or attitude. The main purpose is to redeem them and save their souls. This thought must always be uppermost.

The main effort at this stage is to persuade those persons who are out of line with God's will to straighten matters out of their own free will. They must be clearly convinced of their wrong, and the one counseling them must be absolutely certain of his interpretations—otherwise the process will fail. If they see the point clearly and will voluntarily yield to the teaching, this will clear it all up.

# Discipline

For those who are guilty and will not repent, after every possible effort has been made to get them to do so, the only option left is to withdraw fellowship.

In 1 Corinthians 5:1-13 we have certain instruction on what the church must do with known fornicators. This action (cf. vv. 2, 5, 7, 9, 13) is to be done for the good of the individual himself (v. 5) in the hopes of saving him.

The demand for withdrawal of fellowship is not limited to fornicators, but as v. 11 shows, it also includes the greedy, idolators, revilers, drunkards and robbers.

In Matthew 18:15-17 we find other teaching that gives advice with respect to the withdrawal of fellowship. Here the problem begins with one brother sinning against another. After due entreaties and admonitions (with definite guilt clearly understood) when the guilty brother refuses to repent he should be withdrawn from.

The above passages and teachings furnish adequate patterns and authority for the withdrawal of fellowship. Good judgment will determine the local application for various cases.

In no instance should withdrawal of fellowship be personally vindictive. It should be preceded by many prayers and efforts to persuade the party to come to repentance. Finally an *oral* public statement should be made of the formal withdrawal, giving scriptural justification and just enough history of the case to show that this is a necessary action and that many efforts to bring reconciliation have failed.

After withdrawal all brethren should avoid social fellowship with the withdrawee, in hopes that the ostracization will cause repentance. (1 Corinthians 5:9, 11).

Good judgment, based upon a full knowledge of the scripture plus a full knowledge of the facts of the case in hand is the ideal to be sought.

Bad judgment has been shown in the past by some leaders in these ways:

1. Playing favorites. Being more indulgent with friends, or relatives than with others.

2. Having a personal axe to grind.

3. Allowing meddlers who do not belong in any counseling aspect of the case, to try to regulate the lives of others.

4. Discussing details of the case (either during or after the solution) with persons other than those involved or other counselors. The closed-mouth is necessary here.

5. Being too authority-conscious and thus being dictatorial. The elder must realize that he has no obligation to assume God's role.

6. Trying to force people to do God's will. Some people simply choose not to do so.

7. Failing to rely on prayer.

As a closing thought, we wish to invite your attention to the following statement of policy recently issued by the elders of the Madison, Tennessee congregation to their members:

## A STATEMENT OF POLICY

Among responsibilities vested in the eldership, none exceeds in weight—and sometimes heartbreak—that of exercising Bible-directed discipline upon the erring. Kindness and patience always are in order, but corrective treatment is mandatory for members who willfully and knowingly persist in sinful misconduct.

Whatever the nature of the iniquity, the obligation is there. For guarding the flock, like feeding spiritually, is a primary duty assigned. To ignore a known delinquency—to seemingly condone it—is not a kindness. It is a default for which the elders would have to answer in the judgment.

The Lord's instructions on this point are clear: To handle responsibility any cases of flagrant misconduct that occur. No member of this eldership would treat it recklessly. We cannot, however, close our eyes to any matter that brings reproach upon the church.

Seldom in the forty-three year history of this congregation has it been necessary to exercise the extreme step of disfellowshipping. Upon occasion, however, it has been—and doubtless will be again.

A congregation rooted and grounded in the truth knows what the obligations are—on the part of the elders and the members. The purpose always is to REDEEM—not recriminate.

We are accountable in God's sight for stewardship, and answerable if by neglect we have permitted souls, unwarned, to go astray.

Dangers are compounded in an age of increasing wantonness—when influences of moral degradation beat upon our society; when so-called "Situation Ethics" are proposed to supplant Christian moral standards, and confront even stalwart Christian families with perils of temptation. The church can and must stand as a dike—a tower of spiritual strength against that tide. But it can do that only if courage and judgment equal the demands of Christian conscience on the part of its stewards.

The elders at Madison are sensitive to that responsibility in an assignment relating to the eternal welfare of human souls.

In Christian love always, and in the kindest way we know, we shall keep the faith.

—The Elders

## STUDY QUESTIONS

### Chapter 13

1. Why have elders not been diligent in the matter of church discipline?

2. Outline and discuss methods of teaching in the matter of divorce and remarriage.

3. What value is there to formal study of ways to improve even good marriages?

4. Discuss and evaluate some counseling attitudes. What is wrong with authoritarianism?

5. Comment on the importance of elders being perpetual students.

6. Why is thoroughness in "fact gathering" important?

7. Discuss the persuasion factor.

8. Give the basic biblical teaching on the withdrawal of fellowship. List some cautions in applying it.

9. List some ways in which bad judgment may be used by leaders.

10. How important is courage in a leader? What should it be tempered with?

# NOTES

[To avoid dealing in personalities any more than necessary, a source referred to in the notes will be identified only by its Bibliography Number.]

[1] 20–pp. 48, 49

[2] When fornication is considered as the only ground for divorce approved by God it is considered that the sin is committed *after* the marriage, not *before,* by practically all commentators. The assumption seems to be that when one marries a spouse he accepts her (or him) as "having a clean slate" at the time.

[3] 20–p. 45

[4] 3–March 6, 1952, p. 152

[5] 20–p. 54

[6] 20–pp. 53, 54

[7] "restoration" means to restore New Testament Christianity.

[8] 20–pp. 4, 5, 43

[9] 20–p. 4

[10] Ibid.

[11] Ibid.

[12] Ibid.

[13] 3–July 26, 1952, p. 471

[14] Ibid.

[15] 7–p. 276, No. 1291

[16] 10–p. 11

[17] 20–p. 45

[18] 20–p. 46

[19] 20–p. 49

[20] 9

[21] 9, p. 28

[22] 9, pp. 29, 30

[23] 9, p. 30

[24] For the basic argument and ideas given here as replies, we wish to acknowledge credit to Roy Deaver, whose article in the January, 1975 issue of the *Spiritual Sword* is somewhat definitive, in our judgment.

[25] 5, Jan. 1975, p. 22

[26] It is our understanding that the "handcuff" illustration was first used by Andrew Connally (*Spiritual Sword,* Vol. 3, No. 1, Oct. 1971, p. 48), and this is what is here reacted to. Deaver's more elaborate illustration came later.

[27] 9, p. 22

[28] 6, p. 38

[29] 2, pp. 100-102

[30] Among the suggestions given for the sort of bondage the Christian is freed from are–bondage to:
   a. "Live with the spouse and provide conjugal rights."
   b. "Try to force the law of Christianity upon a reluctant spouse."
   c. "The marriage state, and thus not required to sacrifice one's self-respect and domestic quiet, for the purpose of leading an unbelieving husband or wife to the truth."
   d. "Live under a morbid sense of duty, to  preserve the spouse from perdition, and yet still be under conjugal obligations."
   e. "Be enslaved, in a way that would require one to participate in idolatry or be in a position of groveling to the unbelieving spouse."
   f. "Be enslaved, which would be the opposite of 'peace' in the context."
   g. "Refuse to be set free, or try to prevent the divorce at the cost of all liberty."

[31] 13, pp. 179-180

[32] If an innocent person has been put away, NOT for fornication but unjustly, and his separated spouse later commits adultery or remarries, he would himself then have scriptural grounds for divorce and remarriage.

# BIBLIOGRAPHY

1. Arndt, W. F., and Gingrich, F. W., *A Greek-English Lexicon of the New Testament*, Chicago: University of Chicago Press, 1952.

2. Brewer, G. C., *Contending For the Faith*, Nashville: Gospel Advocate Company, 1941, pp. 57-102.

3. Brewer, G. C., Articles in *Gospel Advocate*, June 28, 1951; July 26, 1951; August 16, 1951; February 7, 1952; March 6 and 20, 1952.

4. Dana, H. E., and Mantey, J. R., *A Manual Grammar of the Greek New Testament*, New York: MacMillan, 1941, pp. 181-186.

5. Deaver, Roy, Articles in *Spiritual Sword*, April 1972, p. 9; and January, 1975, p. 14.

6. Floyd, Harvey, Article in *Spiritual Sword*, January 1975, p. 37.

7. Goodwin, W. W., *Greek Grammar*, Rev. Ed., No Publisher, 1892.

8. Greenfield, Wm., *A Greek-English Lexicon to the New Testament*, New York: Harper, n. d.

9. Hale, Lewis G., *Except For Fornication,* Oklahoma City: Hale Publications, 1974.

10. Hall, Michael, "Ministering To the Divorced," *Mission,* Vol. 10, No. 8, February 1977, p. 10-12.

11. Hovey, Alva, *The Scriptural Law of Divorce,* Phila: American Baptist Publication Society, 1866.

12. Lanier, Roy H. Sr., Article in *Spiritual Sword,* January 1975, p. 33.

13. Roberts, R. L. Jr., "The Meaning of *Chōrizō* and *Douloō* in 1 Corinthians 7:10-17," *Restoration Quarterly,* Vol. 8, No. 3, 3rd Quarter, 1965, **pp. 179-184.**

14. Schubert, Joe D., *Marriage Divorce and Purity,* Way of Life series No. 101, Abilene: Biblical Research Press, 1966.

15. Shelly, Rubel, Article in *Spiritual Sword,* January 1975, p. 39.

16. Trench, R. C., *Synonyms of the Greek New Testament,* Eerdmans Reprint.

17. Vincent, M. R., *Word Studies,* Vol. 3, New York: Scribner's, 1902.

18. Warpula, Calvin, Articles in *Firm Foundation,* March 1 and 8, 1977.

19. Warren, Thomas B., Editorials in *Spiritual Sword,* April 1972 and January 1975.

20. Woodruff, James S., *The Divorce Dilemma,* Nashville: Christian Family Books, 1973.